R E A D E R ' S   G U I D E

TO

The Great Gatsby

READER'S GUIDE

TO

The Great Gatsby

Selected and Edited by

Nancy Carr
Joseph Coulson
Anne Gendler
Mike Levine

Published by the Great Books Foundation

A nonprofit educational organization

Published and distributed by

The Great Books Foundation
A nonprofit educational organization

35 East Wacker Drive, Suite 2300
Chicago, IL 60601-2298
www.greatbooks.org

This edition published by arrangement with
Scribner, an imprint of Simon & Schuster, Inc.

First printing
9 8 7 6 5 4 3 2 1 0

Library of Congress Cataloging-in-Publication Data

Reader's guide to The Great Gatsby.
        p. cm.
  Includes bibliographical references.
  ISBN 1-880323-87-7 (pbk.)
    1. Fitzgerald, F. Scott (Francis Scott), 1896–1940. Great Gatsby—Handbooks, manuals, etc.
  I. Great Books Foundation (U.S.)
PS3511.I9 G8737 2001
813'.52—dc21   2001033715

Book cover and design:
William Seabright & Associates

About the Great Books Foundation

What is the Great Books Foundation?

The Great Books Foundation is an independent, nonprofit educational organization whose mission is to help people learn how to think and share ideas. Toward this end, the Foundation offers workshops for leaders of and participants in Shared Inquiry Discussion and publishes collections of classic and modern texts for both children and adults.

The Great Books Foundation was established in 1947 to promote liberal education for the general public. In 1962, the Foundation extended its mission to children with the introduction of Junior Great Books. Since its inception, the Foundation has helped thousands of people throughout the United States and in other countries begin their own discussion groups in schools, libraries, and community centers. Today, Foundation instructors conduct thousands of workshops each year, in which educators and parents learn to lead Shared Inquiry Discussion.

What resources are available to support my participation in Shared Inquiry?

The Great Books Foundation offers workshops in Shared Inquiry to help people get the most from discussion. Participants learn how to read actively, pose fruitful questions, and listen and respond to others effectively in discussion. All participants also practice leading a discussion and have an opportunity to reflect on the process with others. For more information about Great Books materials or workshops, call the Great Books Foundation at 1-800-222-5870 or visit our Web site at www.greatbooks.org.

Contents

Introduction

As you read *The Great Gatsby,* by F. Scott Fitzgerald, do you find the novel full of mystery and something of a riddle—like Gatsby himself? Even the most experienced readers and critics have this reaction; indeed, it is our doubts and curiosity that show us where to begin our search for meaning in the text. At the Great Books Foundation, we believe that the best way to come to a fuller understanding of a literary work is to note the things that puzzle you as you read, then develop questions based on your notes and discuss them with others who have read the same text and have questions of their own. We call this method of reading and discussion Shared Inquiry. Your group discussion will yield many possible answers to the questions you have raised, and although you may not come to a definitive conclusion, together you will explore many more possibilities more thoroughly than any one reader could alone.

All readers bring a wealth of background knowledge and personal experience to their encounter with a book. To increase your relevant background knowledge and to sharpen the skills that enable you to better understand how a text achieves its effects, this Reader's Guide provides a biography of the author, Fitzgerald's short story "Winter Dreams," passages from *The Great Gatsby* for close reading, nonfiction that sets Fitzgerald's work in the historical context of America in the 1920s, a glossary of literary terms, and a bibliography with resources for further reading. We hope these materials help make your discussions worthwhile and your encounter with *The Great Gatsby* a rewarding one.

About Shared Inquiry Discussion

Shared Inquiry is the effort to achieve a more thorough understanding of a text by discussing questions, responses, and insights with others. For both the leader and the participants, careful listening is essential. The leader guides the discussion by asking questions about specific ideas and problems of meaning in the text, but does not seek to impose his or her own interpretation on the group.

During a Shared Inquiry Discussion, group members consider a number of possible ideas and weigh the evidence for each. Ideas that are entertained and then refined or abandoned are not thought of as mistakes, but as valuable parts of the thinking process. Group members gain experience in communicating complex ideas and in supporting, testing, and expanding their thoughts. Everyone in the group contributes to the discussion, and while participants may disagree with each other, they treat each other's ideas respectfully.

This process of communal discovery is vital to developing an understanding of important texts and ideas, rather than merely cataloging knowledge about them. By reading and thinking together about important works, you and the other members of your group are joining a great conversation that extends across the centuries.

Guidelines for leading and participating in discussion

Over the past fifty years, the Great Books Foundation has developed guidelines that distill the experience of many discussion groups, with participants of all ages. We have found that when groups follow the procedures outlined below, discussions are most focused and fruitful.

1. **Read the selection before participating in the discussion.** This ensures that all participants are equally prepared to talk about the ideas in the work, and helps prevent talk that would distract the group from its purpose.

2. **Support your ideas with evidence from the text.** This keeps the discussion focused on understanding the selection and enables the group to weigh textual support for different answers and to choose intelligently among them.

3. **Discuss the ideas in the selection, and try to understand them fully before exploring issues that go beyond the selection.** Reflecting on a range of ideas and the evidence to support them makes the exploration of related issues more productive.

4. **Listen to others and respond to them directly.** Shared Inquiry is about the give-and-take of ideas, a willingness to listen to others and to talk to them respectfully. Directing your comments and questions to other group members, not always to the leader, will make the discussion livelier and more dynamic.

5. **Expect the leader to ask questions, rather than answer them.** The leader is a kind of chief learner, whose role is to keep discussion effective and interesting by listening and asking questions. The leader's goal is to help the participants develop their own ideas, with everyone (the leader included) gaining a new understanding in the process. When participants hang back and wait for the leader to suggest answers, discussion falters.

How to make discussions more effective

- **Ask questions when something is unclear.** Simply asking someone to explain what he or she means by a particular word, or to repeat a comment, can give everyone in the group time to think about the idea in depth.

- **Ask for evidence.** Asking "What in the text gave you that idea?" helps everyone better understand the reasoning behind an answer, and it allows the group to consider which ideas have the best support.

- **Ask for agreement and disagreement.** "Does your idea agree with hers, or is it different?" Questions of this kind help the group understand how ideas are related or distinct.

- **Reflect on discussion afterward.** Sharing comments about how the discussion went and ideas for improvement can make each discussion better than the last.

Room arrangement and group size

Ideally, everyone in a discussion should be able to see and hear everyone else. When it isn't possible to arrange the seating in a circle or horseshoe, encourage group members to look at the person talking, acknowledging each other and not just the leader.

In general, Shared Inquiry Discussion is most effective in groups of ten to twenty participants. If a group is much bigger than twenty, it is important to ensure that everyone has a chance to speak. This can be accomplished by either dividing the group in half for discussion or by setting aside time at the end of discussion to go around the room and give each person a chance to make a brief final comment.

Using the Reader's Guide

"Winter Dreams" by F. Scott Fitzgerald

"Winter Dreams" was chosen for its thematic connection to *The Great Gatsby*. Using the questions provided, readers can discuss this short story apart from the novel or as an introduction to some of the novel's ideas and themes. Discussing the story either before or after reading the novel provides an excellent opportunity for comparative analysis.

Interpretive Questions for Discussion of *The Great Gatsby*

Discussion gives participants of all ages an opportunity to express their ideas, listen to the perspectives of others, and synthesize different viewpoints to reach a deeper, more informed understanding of the novel. Effective questions help participants talk specifically about the content and language of the novel, arrange details in logical order, and support their ideas with evidence from the text and personal experience.

Passages and Questions for Close Reading

Passages from *The Great Gatsby* and related questions can be discussed in large and small groups or can be used for individual study and written response. The questions ask the reader to analyze specific literary themes, techniques, and terms as part of the interpretive process.

All readers will benefit from the challenges these questions pose. *Students in honors courses or courses qualifying for college credit will find these questions useful for exam preparation.*

Suggestions for Writing

Postdiscussion writing gives students the opportunity to consider new ideas and measure them against their personal experience and opinions. In these extended writing pieces, students can return to questions not fully resolved in discussion or investigate unexplored avenues of inquiry. Because thorough discussion requires such extensive engagement with the novel, students are better prepared to present their ideas clearly and persuasively or, in the more creative writing assignments, to produce a more fully imagined response.

Background and Context

These selections place the novel and its author in their historical context. Documents about Prohibition, flappers, jazz, and the leisure class, along with other aspects of the Roaring Twenties, will give readers a feel for the world in which Fitzgerald lived and wrote.

When used in the classroom, these selections invite teachers and students in English and history to join forces in discussion of *The Great Gatsby,* examining the social, cultural, and political climate from which the novel emerged.

About the Author

Francis Scott Key Fitzgerald was born on September 24, 1896, in St. Paul, Minnesota. His father, Edward Fitzgerald, came from a distinguished Maryland family but had himself fallen on hard times. Edward had the manners of a perfect Southern gentleman, but he was incapable of earning enough money to live like one. He married a rich woman, Mary (Mollie) McQuillan, whose Irish-immigrant father had become very successful in the wholesale grocery business. Fitzgerald was embarrassed of his mother because she spoiled him, was eccentric, and was a careless dresser. Caught between old breeding and new money, Fitzgerald became class-conscious at a very early age.

His family lived in what Fitzgerald called "a house below the average of a street above the average." Throughout his academic career Fitzgerald attended private schools, but his boasting and lack of athleticism often made him unpopular. Accordingly, he decided to find other ways to become popular and respected. He began writing stories and plays while still in elementary school, usually in the blank pages of his textbooks during class time, and published several writings in school magazines. During school vacations, two of his plays were performed as fundraisers and were successes.

In the fall of 1913, Fitzgerald enrolled at Princeton University, which he saw as an opportunity to prove that "life was something you dominated if you were any good." He was cut from the football team but gained a certain amount of fame as a writer; he wrote musical comedies for the Triangle Club, a campus theater group, followed by stories and poems for *The Tiger* and the *Nassau Literary Magazine,* Princeton's literary publications. Two of his closest friends were Edmund Wilson, who later became a well-known literary critic and Fitzgerald's "intellectual conscience," and John Peale Bishop, a poet. During Christmas vacation of his sophomore year, Fitzgerald met and fell in love with Ginevra King, a beautiful, popular, and ultimately unattainable debutante who became the model for many of his heroines, including Judy Jones in his short story "Winter Dreams."

Fitzgerald continued writing instead of studying and enlisted in the army in 1917 to avoid flunking out of Princeton. He had hoped to fight overseas in World War I but instead was trapped in officer training in Fort Leavenworth, Kansas. He began writing a novel, *The Romantic Egotist,* and submitted it to Scribner's. The publisher rejected it, but one of the editors, Maxwell Perkins, liked the manuscript well enough to ask Fitzgerald to make revisions and resubmit it.

In the summer of 1918, Fitzgerald was transferred to Camp Sheridan, near Montgomery, Alabama. At a country club dance, he met Zelda Sayre, the belle of Montgomery, and fell deeply in love; soon they were engaged. Zelda was beautiful, brilliant, and artistic, and she grew bored very easily. "I was in love with a whirlwind," Fitzgerald wrote later, "and I must spin a net big enough to catch it out of my head, a head full of trickling nickels and sliding dimes, the incessant music box of the poor."

Fitzgerald decided to move to New York to make a fortune with which he

F. Scott and Zelda Fitzgerald with their daughter, Scottie, in France, December 1925

could support Zelda. However, after six months of working at an advertising firm, he was still poor, had sold only one story, was drinking too much, and was no longer engaged, because Zelda did not want to wait for him to become rich and well known. In the summer of 1919, he moved back into his parents' house in St. Paul and finished rewriting his novel. This time, Scribner's accepted it. Maxwell Perkins was his editor and would remain so for the rest of Fitzgerald's life. *This Side of Paradise* was published on March 26, 1920. It became an immediate bestseller and fascinated readers with its depiction of youthful college experiences. A week later, Fitzgerald and Zelda were married in New York; at last, as he later wrote, reflecting on the realization of his dreams, "the fulfilled future and the wistful past were mingled in a single gorgeous moment."

The Fitzgeralds embodied the spirit of the Jazz Age. They did "what they had always wanted to" and enjoyed themselves in New York, diving into the fountain at the Plaza Hotel and riding down Fifth Avenue on the hoods of taxicabs. Seventeen years later, Fitzgerald would write that "premature success gives one an almost mystical conception of destiny as opposed to will power."

Although *This Side of Paradise* continued to sell, Fitzgerald began writing short stories for magazines, such as *The Saturday Evening Post,* to pay the bills. He wrote a second novel, *The Beautiful and Damned,* which was less successful than its predecessor. In 1921, the Fitzgeralds' daughter, Frances Scott (known as Scottie), was born. The family moved the next year to Great Neck on Long Island, where Fitzgerald worked on his play *The Vegetable* amid a series of wild weekend parties.

After *The Vegetable* flopped in 1923, Fitzgerald began work on the novel that would become *The Great Gatsby*. He told Maxwell Perkins, "I want to write something new—something extraordinary and beautiful and simple and intricately patterned." At the time Fitzgerald began writing *The Great Gatsby,* he was influenced by the works of Joseph Conrad and Henry James, notably Conrad's assertion that a work of art contains its own justification in every line. The setting of *The Great Gatsby* came directly from Fitzgerald's life in Great Neck, and he drew on his courtship of Zelda for the early romance of Daisy and Gatsby. Daisy was the unattainable dream girl, much like Ginevra was and Zelda might have been had *This Side of Paradise* not been a success. Though Gatsby's rise to fortune was based on the 1922 collapse of stockbroker E. M. Fuller, and the character himself "was perhaps created in the image of some forgotten farm type of Minnesota," Gatsby's romanticism was Fitzgerald's, as was Nick Carraway's fascination with life in the East. *The Great Gatsby* was published in the spring of 1925 to some of the best reviews of Fitzgerald's career.

In 1924, the Fitzgeralds moved to France, where they could "live on practically nothing a year." Many American expatriates lived there at the time, most notably Gerald and Sara Murphy, a wealthy and elegant couple whom Fitzgerald befriended, and Ernest Hemingway, who was working as a newspaper reporter and had just published his first book of short stories. Fitzgerald admired both Hemingway and his writing and introduced Hemingway to Perkins, who accepted his first novel, *The Sun Also Rises*.

In Europe, Fitzgerald continued to have problems with his drinking, occasionally remaining drunk for days at a time, and he and Zelda fought constantly. The drinking and fighting began to interfere with his work. He started to write a new novel but ran into trouble, repeatedly interrupting his work to write short stories to get himself and Zelda out of debt. The couple returned to America at the end of 1926, and Fitzgerald went to Hollywood to try to earn some quick money as a screenwriter. His script, however, did not sell, and the family moved to Delaware so Fitzgerald could continue work on his novel. But they had trouble settling down—Fitzgerald could not write, and Zelda had suddenly decided to become a professional dancer and had begun practicing obsessively—so they returned to Paris for the summer of 1928.

Fitzgerald later believed Zelda's dancing was one of the early signs of her growing insanity, but she did not suffer a complete breakdown until the spring of 1930. It was the first of three breakdowns. Doctors diagnosed Zelda as schizophrenic, and she spent the rest of her life in and out of mental institutions.

Tender Is the Night, Fitzgerald's last completed novel, was published in 1934. He based the novel on his and Zelda's experiences in France with the Murphys and in the Swiss clinic where Zelda stayed after her first breakdown. The novel received mediocre reviews and did not sell. Zelda grew worse, their debts piled up, and the magazines were no longer paying top dollar for stories. In 1936, Fitzgerald wrote a series of essays for *Esquire,* the "Crack-Up" articles, in which he described what he termed "emotional bankruptcy." He wrote, "The natural state of the sentient adult is a qualified unhappiness. . . . I think that my happiness, or talent for self-delusion or what you will, was an exception. It was not the natural thing but the unnatural—unnatural as the Boom; and my recent experience parallels the wave of despair that swept the nation when the Boom was over."

Fitzgerald moved to Hollywood in 1937 to write for the movies and lived there for the rest of his life. He was not a success, receiving only one screen credit in three years. He continued to drink heavily, which led to a series of humiliations at Hollywood parties and even the loss of some writing jobs. He made repeated and unsuccessful attempts to quit drinking. At a party one week after he arrived in Hollywood, Fitzgerald met the London-born gossip columnist Sheilah Graham, whom he fell in love with and lived with until he died.

While in Hollywood, Fitzgerald continued to write short stories and began work on *The Last Tycoon,* a novel based on the life of movie producer Irving Thalberg. The head of a major movie studio by the time he was twenty, Thalberg died before he was forty. Some critics believe that, had Fitzgerald finished it, *The Last Tycoon* would have been a major American novel.

Fitzgerald died of a heart attack on December 21, 1940. In 1947, Zelda died in a fire at the mental institution where she was living. While *The Great Gatsby* was not out of print when Fitzgerald died, it was certainly not considered the classic it is today. In 1941, however, Fitzgerald's old friend Edmund Wilson published the uncompleted manuscript and notes for *The Last Tycoon,* and in 1945,

Scott and Zelda in the early 1920s

he edited a collection of Fitzgerald's "Crack-Up" essays and unpublished works, which revived the public's interest in Fitzgerald and his earlier writing. The first of several critical biographies appeared in 1951; in addition to Wilson's efforts, this also led to a renewed appreciation of Fitzgerald's work and helped assure his reputation as one of the greatest American authors of the twentieth century.

This story was published in 1922, three years
before *The Great Gatsby*.

Winter Dreams

F. Scott Fitzgerald

I

Some of the caddies were poor as sin and lived in one-room houses with a neurasthenic cow in the front yard, but Dexter Green's father owned the second-best grocery store in Black Bear—the best one was "The Hub," patronized by the wealthy people from Sherry Island—and Dexter caddied only for pocket money.

In the fall when the days became crisp and gray, and the long Minnesota winter shut down like the white lid of a box, Dexter's skis moved over the snow that hid the fairways of the golf course. At these times the country gave him a feeling of profound melancholy—it offended him that the links should lie in enforced fallowness, haunted by ragged sparrows for the long season. It was dreary, too, that on the tees where the gay colors fluttered in summer there were now only the desolate sandboxes knee-deep in crusted ice. When he crossed the hills the wind blew cold as misery, and if the sun was out he tramped with his eyes squinted up against the hard dimensionless glare.

In April the winter ceased abruptly. The snow ran down into Black Bear Lake scarcely tarrying for the early golfers to brave the season with red and black balls. Without elation, without an interval of moist glory, the cold was gone.

Dexter knew that there was something dismal about this northern spring, just as he knew there was something gorgeous about the fall. Fall made him clench his hands and tremble and repeat idiotic sentences to himself, and make brisk abrupt gestures of command to imaginary audiences and armies. October filled him with hope which November raised to a sort of ecstatic triumph, and in this mood the fleeting brilliant impressions of the summer at Sherry Island were ready grist to his mill. He became a golf champion and defeated Mr. T. A. Hedrick in a marvelous match played a hundred times over the fairways of his imagination, a match each detail of which he changed about untiringly—sometimes he won with almost laughable ease, sometimes he came up magnificently from behind. Again, stepping from a Pierce-Arrow automobile, like Mr. Mortimer Jones, he strolled frigidly into the lounge of the Sherry Island Golf Club—or perhaps, surrounded by an admiring crowd, he gave an exhibition of fancy diving from the springboard of the club raft. . . . Among those who watched him in open-mouthed wonder was Mr. Mortimer Jones.

And one day it came to pass that Mr. Jones—himself and not his ghost—came up to Dexter with tears in his eyes and said that Dexter was the —— best caddy in the club, and wouldn't he decide not to quit if Mr. Jones made it worth his while, because every other —— caddy in the club lost one ball a hole for him—regularly—

"No, sir," said Dexter decisively, "I don't want to caddy anymore." Then, after a pause: "I'm too old."

"You're not more than fourteen. Why the devil did you decide just this morning that you wanted to quit? You promised that next week you'd go over to the state tournament with me."

"I decided I was too old."

Dexter handed in his "A Class" badge, collected what money was due him from the caddy-master, and walked home to Black Bear Village.

"The best —— caddy I ever saw," shouted Mr. Mortimer Jones over a drink that afternoon. "Never lost a ball! Willing! Intelligent! Quiet! Honest! Grateful!"

The little girl who had done this was eleven—beautifully ugly as little girls are apt to be who are destined after a few years to be inexpressibly lovely and bring no end of misery to a great number of men. The spark, however, was perceptible. There was a general ungodliness in the way her lips twisted down at the corners when she smiled, and in the—Heaven help us!—in the almost passionate quality of her eyes. Vitality is born in such women. It was utterly in evidence now, shining through her thin frame in a sort of glow.

She had come eagerly out onto the course at nine o'clock with a white linen nurse and five small new golfclubs in a white canvas bag which the nurse was carrying. When Dexter first saw her she was standing by the caddy house, rather ill at ease and trying to conceal the fact by engaging her nurse in an obviously unnatural conversation graced by startling and irrelevant grimaces from herself.

"Well, it's certainly a nice day, Hilda," Dexter heard her say. She drew down the corners of her mouth, smiled, and glanced furtively around, her eyes in transit falling for an instant on Dexter.

Then to the nurse:

"Well, I guess there aren't very many people out here this morning, are there?"

The smile again—radiant, blatantly artificial—convincing.

"I don't know what we're supposed to do now," said the nurse, looking nowhere in particular.

"Oh, that's all right. I'll fix it up."

Dexter stood perfectly still, his mouth slightly ajar. He knew that if he moved forward a step his stare would be in her line of vision—if he moved backward he would lose his full view of her face. For a moment he had not realized how young she was. Now he remembered having seen her several times the year before—in bloomers.

Suddenly, involuntarily, he laughed, a short abrupt laugh—then, startled by himself, he turned and began to walk quickly away.

"Boy!"

Dexter stopped.

"Boy—"

Beyond question he was addressed. Not only that, but he was treated to that absurd smile, that preposterous smile—the memory of which at least a dozen men were to carry into middle age.

"Boy, do you know where the golf teacher is?"

"He's giving a lesson."

"Well, do you know where the caddy-master is?"

"He isn't here yet this morning."

"Oh." For a moment this baffled her. She stood alternately on her right and left foot.

"We'd like to get a caddy," said the nurse. "Mrs. Mortimer Jones sent us out to play golf, and we don't know how without we get a caddy."

Here she was stopped by an ominous glance from Miss Jones, followed immediately by the smile.

"There aren't any caddies here except me," said Dexter to the nurse, "and I got to stay here in charge until the caddy-master gets here."

"Oh."

Miss Jones and her retinue now withdrew, and at a proper distance from Dexter became involved in a heated conversation, which was concluded by Miss Jones taking one of the clubs and hitting it on the ground with violence. For further emphasis she raised it again and was about to bring it down smartly upon the nurse's bosom, when the nurse seized the club and twisted it from her hands.

"You damn little mean old *thing!*" cried Miss Jones wildly.

Another argument ensued. Realizing that the elements of comedy were implied in the scene, Dexter several times began to laugh, but each time restrained the laugh before it reached audibility. He could not resist the monstrous conviction that the little girl was justified in beating the nurse.

The situation was resolved by the fortuitous appearance of the caddy-master, who was appealed to immediately by the nurse.

"Miss Jones is to have a little caddy, and this one says he can't go."

"Mr. McKenna said I was to wait here till you came," said Dexter quickly.

"Well, he's here now." Miss Jones smiled cheerfully at the caddy-master. Then she dropped her bag and set off at a haughty mince toward the first tee.

"Well?" The caddy-master turned to Dexter. "What you standing there like a dummy for? Go pick up the young lady's clubs."

"I don't think I'll go out today," said Dexter.

"You don't—"

"I think I'll quit."

The enormity of his decision frightened him. He was a favorite caddy, and the thirty dollars a month he earned through the summer were not to be made elsewhere around the lake. But he had received a strong emotional shock, and his perturbation required a violent and immediate outlet.

It is not so simple as that, either. As so frequently would be the case in the future, Dexter was unconsciously dictated to by his winter dreams.

II

Now, of course, the quality and the seasonability of these winter dreams varied, but the stuff of them remained. They persuaded Dexter several years later to pass up a business course at the state university—his father, prospering now, would have paid his way—for the precarious advantage of attending an older and more famous university in the East, where he was bothered by his scanty funds. But do not get the impression, because his winter dreams happened to be concerned at first with musings on the rich, that there was anything merely snobbish in the boy. He wanted not association with glittering things and glittering people—he wanted the glittering things themselves. Often he reached out for the best without knowing why he wanted it—and sometimes he ran up against the mysterious denials and prohibitions in which life indulges. It is with one of those denials and not with his career as a whole that this story deals.

He made money. It was rather amazing. After college he went to the city from which Black Bear Lake draws its wealthy patrons. When he was only twenty-three and had been there not quite two years, there were already people who liked to say: "Now *there's* a boy—" All about him rich men's sons were peddling bonds precariously, or investing patrimonies precariously, or plodding through the two dozen volumes of the "George Washington Commercial Course," but Dexter borrowed a thousand dollars on his college degree and his confident mouth, and bought a partnership in a laundry.

It was a small laundry when he went into it, but Dexter made a specialty of learning how the English washed fine woolen golf-stockings without shrinking them, and within a year he was catering to the trade that wore knickerbockers. Men were insisting that their Shetland hose and sweaters go to his laundry, just as they had insisted on a caddy who could find golfballs. A little later he was doing their wives' lingerie as well—and running five branches in different parts of the city. Before he was twenty-seven he owned the largest string of laundries in his section of the country. It was then that he sold out and went to New York. But the part of his story that concerns us goes back to the days when he was making his first big success.

When he was twenty-three Mr. Hart—one of the gray-haired men who liked to say "Now there's a boy"—gave him a guest card to the Sherry Island Golf Club for a weekend. So he signed his name one day on the register, and that afternoon played golf in a foursome with Mr. Hart and Mr. Sandwood and Mr. T. A. Hedrick. He did not consider it necessary to remark that he had once carried Mr. Hart's bag over this same links, and that he knew every trap and gully with his eyes shut—but he found himself glancing at the four caddies who trailed them, trying to catch a gleam or gesture that would remind him of himself, that would lessen the gap which lay between his present and his past.

It was a curious day, slashed abruptly with fleeting, familiar impressions. One minute he had the sense of being a trespasser—in the next he was impressed by the tremendous superiority he felt toward Mr. T. A. Hedrick, who was a bore and not even a good golfer anymore.

Then, because of a ball Mr. Hart lost near the fifteenth green, an enormous thing happened. While they were searching the stiff grasses of the rough there was a clear call of "Fore!" from behind a hill in their rear. And as they all turned abruptly from their search a bright new ball sliced abruptly over the hill and caught Mr. T. A. Hedrick in the abdomen.

"By Gad!" cried Mr. T. A. Hedrick, "they ought to put some of these crazy women off the course. It's getting to be outrageous."

A head and a voice came up together over the hill:

"Do you mind if we go through?"

"You hit me in the stomach!" declared Mr. Hedrick wildly.

"Did I?" The girl approached the group of men. "I'm sorry. I yelled 'Fore!' "

Her glance fell casually on each of the men—then scanned the fairway for her ball.

"Did I bounce into the rough?"

It was impossible to determine whether this question was ingenuous or malicious. In a moment, however, she left no doubt, for as her partner came up over the hill she called cheerfully:

"Here I am! I'd have gone on the green except that I hit something."

As she took her stance for a short mashie shot, Dexter looked at her closely. She wore a blue gingham dress, rimmed at throat and shoulders with a white edging that accentuated her tan. The quality of exaggeration, of thinness, which had made her passionate eyes and down-turning mouth absurd at eleven, was gone now. She was arrestingly beautiful. The color in her cheeks was centered like the color in a picture—it was not a "high" color, but a sort of fluctuating and feverish warmth, so shaded that it seemed at any moment it would recede and disappear. This color and the mobility of her mouth gave a continual impression of flux, of intense life, of passionate vitality—balanced only partially by the sad luxury of her eyes.

She swung her mashie impatiently and without interest, pitching the ball into a sandpit on the other side of the green. With a quick, insincere smile and a careless "Thank you!" she went on after it.

"That Judy Jones!" remarked Mr. Hedrick on the next tee, as they waited—some moments—for her to play on ahead. "All she needs is to be turned up and spanked for six months and then to be married off to an old-fashioned cavalry captain."

"My God, she's good-looking!" said Mr. Sandwood, who was just over thirty.

"Good-looking!" cried Mr. Hedrick contemptuously. "She always looks as if she wanted to be kissed! Turning those big cow-eyes on every calf in town!"

It was doubtful if Mr. Hedrick intended a reference to the maternal instinct.

"She'd play pretty good golf if she'd try," said Mr. Sandwood.

"She has no form," said Mr. Hedrick solemnly.

"She has a nice figure," said Mr. Sandwood.

"Better thank the Lord she doesn't drive a swifter ball," said Mr. Hart, winking at Dexter.

Later in the afternoon the sun went down with a riotous swirl of gold and varying blues and scarlets, and left the dry, rustling night of western summer. Dexter watched from the veranda of the Golf Club, watched the even overlap of the waters in the little wind, silver molasses under the harvest moon. Then the moon held a finger to her lips and the lake became a clear pool, pale and quiet. Dexter put on his bathing suit and swam out to the farthest raft, where he stretched dripping on the wet canvas of the springboard.

There was a fish jumping and a star shining and the lights around the lake were gleaming. Over on a dark peninsula a piano was playing the songs of last summer and of summers before that—songs from "Chin-Chin" and "The Count of Luxemburg" and "The Chocolate Soldier"—and because the sound of a piano over a stretch of water had always seemed beautiful to Dexter he lay perfectly quiet and listened.

The tune the piano was playing at that moment had been gay and new five years before when Dexter was a sophomore at college. They had played it at a prom once when he could not afford the luxury of proms, and he had stood outside the gymnasium and listened. The sound of the tune precipitated in him a sort of ecstasy and it was with that ecstasy he viewed what happened to him now. It was a mood of intense appreciation, a sense that, for once, he was magnificently attuned to life and that everything about him was radiating a brightness and a glamour he might never know again.

A low, pale oblong detached itself suddenly from the darkness of the island, spitting forth the reverberated sound of a racing motorboat. Two white streamers of cleft water rolled themselves out behind it and almost immediately the boat was beside him, drowning out the hot tinkle of the piano in the drone of its spray. Dexter, raising himself on his arms, was aware of a figure standing at the wheel, of two dark eyes regarding him over the lengthening space of water— then the boat had gone by and was sweeping in an immense and purposeless circle of spray round and round in the middle of the lake. With equal eccentricity one of the circles flattened out and headed back toward the raft.

"Who's that?" she called, shutting off her motor. She was so near now that Dexter could see her bathing suit, which consisted apparently of pink rompers.

The nose of the boat bumped the raft, and as the latter tilted rakishly he was precipitated toward her. With different degrees of interest they recognized each other.

"Aren't you one of those men we played through this afternoon?" she demanded.

He was.

"Well, do you know how to drive a motorboat? Because if you do I wish you'd drive this one so I can ride on the surfboard behind. My name is Judy Jones"—she favored him with an absurd smirk—rather, what tried to be a smirk, for, twist her mouth as she might, it was not grotesque, it was merely beautiful— "and I live in a house over there on the island, and in that house there is a man waiting for me. When he drove up at the door I drove out of the dock because he says I'm his ideal."

There was a fish jumping and a star shining and the lights around the lake were gleaming. Dexter sat beside Judy Jones and she explained how her boat was driven. Then she was in the water, swimming to the floating surfboard with a sinuous crawl. Watching her was without effort to the eye, watching a branch waving or a seagull flying. Her arms, burned to butternut, moved sinuously among the dull platinum ripples, elbow appearing first, casting the forearm back with a cadence of falling water, then reaching out and down, stabbing a path ahead.

They moved out into the lake, turning. Dexter saw that she was kneeling on the low rear of the now uptilted surfboard.

"Go faster," she called, "fast as it'll go."

Obediently he jammed the lever forward and the white spray mounted at the bow. When he looked around again the girl was standing up on the rushing board, her arms spread wide, her eyes lifted toward the moon.

"It's awful cold," she shouted. "What's your name?"

He told her.

"Well, why don't you come to dinner tomorrow night?"

His heart turned over like the flywheel of the boat, and, for the second time, her casual whim gave a new direction to his life.

III

Next evening while he waited for her to come downstairs, Dexter peopled the soft deep summer room and the sunporch that opened from it with the men who had already loved Judy Jones. He knew the sort of men they were—the men who when he first went to college had entered from the great prep schools with graceful clothes and the deep tan of healthy summers. He had seen that, in one sense, he was better than these men. He was newer and stronger. Yet in acknowledging to himself that he wished his children to be like them he was admitting that he was but the rough, strong stuff from which they eternally sprang.

When the time had come for him to wear good clothes, he had known who were the best tailors in America, and the best tailors in America had made him the suit he wore this evening. He had acquired that particular reserve peculiar to his university, that set it off from other universities. He recognized the value to him of such a mannerism and he had adopted it; he knew that to be careless in dress and manner required more confidence than to be careful. But carelessness was for his children. His mother's name had been Krimplich. She was a Bohemian of the peasant class and she had talked broken English to the end of her days. Her son must keep to the set patterns.

At a little after seven Judy Jones came downstairs. She wore a blue silk afternoon dress, and he was disappointed at first that she had not put on something more elaborate. This feeling was accentuated when, after a brief greeting,

25

she went to the door of a butler's pantry and, pushing it open, called: "You can serve dinner, Martha." He had rather expected that a butler would announce dinner, that there would be a cocktail. Then he put these thoughts behind him as they sat down side by side on a lounge and looked at each other.

"Father and Mother won't be here," she said thoughtfully.

He remembered the last time he had seen her father, and he was glad the parents were not to be here tonight—they might wonder who he was. He had been born in Keeble, a Minnesota village fifty miles farther north, and he always gave Keeble as his home instead of Black Bear Village. Country towns were well enough to come from if they weren't inconveniently in sight and used as footstools by fashionable lakes.

They talked of his university, which she had visited frequently during the past two years, and of the nearby city which supplied Sherry Island with its patrons, and whither Dexter would return next day to his prospering laundries.

During dinner she slipped into a moody depression which gave Dexter a feeling of uneasiness. Whatever petulance she uttered in her throaty voice worried him. Whatever she smiled at—at him, at a chicken liver, at nothing—it disturbed him that her smile could have no root in mirth, or even in amusement. When the scarlet corners of her lips curved down, it was less a smile than an invitation to a kiss.

Then, after dinner, she led him out on the dark sunporch and deliberately changed the atmosphere.

"Do you mind if I weep a little?" she said.

"I'm afraid I'm boring you," he responded quickly.

"You're not. I like you. But I've just had a terrible afternoon. There was a man I cared about, and this afternoon he told me out of a clear sky that he was poor as a church mouse. He'd never even hinted it before. Does this sound horribly mundane?"

"Perhaps he was afraid to tell you."

"Suppose he was," she answered. "He didn't start right. You see, if I'd thought of him as poor—well, I've been mad about loads of poor men, and fully intended to marry them all. But in this case, I hadn't thought of him that way, and my interest in him wasn't strong enough to survive the shock. As if a girl calmly informed her fiancé that she was a widow. He might not object to widows, but—

"Let's start right," she interrupted herself suddenly. "Who are you, anyhow?"
For a moment Dexter hesitated. Then:

"I'm nobody," he announced. "My career is largely a matter of futures."

"Are you poor?"

"No," he said frankly, "I'm probably making more money than any man my age in the Northwest. I know that's an obnoxious remark, but you advised me to start right."

There was a pause. Then she smiled and the corners of her mouth drooped and an almost imperceptible sway brought her closer to him, looking up into his eyes. A lump rose in Dexter's throat, and he waited breathless for the experiment, facing the unpredictable compound that would form mysteriously from the elements of their lips. Then he saw—she communicated her excitement to him, lavishly, deeply, with kisses that were not a promise but a fulfillment. They aroused in him not hunger demanding renewal but surfeit that would demand more surfeit . . . kisses that were like charity, creating want by holding back nothing at all.

It did not take him many hours to decide that he had wanted Judy Jones ever since he was a proud, desirous little boy.

IV

It began like that—and continued, with varying shades of intensity, on such a note right up to the dénouement. Dexter surrendered a part of himself to the most direct and unprincipled personality with which he had ever come in contact. Whatever Judy wanted, she went after with the full pressure of her charm. There was no divergence of method, no jockeying for position or premeditation of effects—there was very little mental side to any of her affairs. She simply made men conscious to the highest degree of her physical loveliness. Dexter had no desire to change her. Her deficiencies were knit up with a passionate energy that transcended and justified them.

When, as Judy's head lay against his shoulder that first night, she whispered, "I don't know what's the matter with me. Last night I thought I was in love with a man and tonight I think I'm in love with you—" it seemed to him a beautiful and romantic thing to say. It was the exquisite excitability that for the moment he controlled and owned. But a week later he was compelled to view this same quality in a different light. She took him in her roadster to a picnic supper, and after supper she disappeared, likewise in her roadster, with another man. Dexter became enormously upset and was scarcely able to be decently civil to the other people present. When she assured him that she had not kissed the other man, he knew she was lying—yet he was glad that she had taken the trouble to lie to him.

He was, as he found before the summer ended, one of a varying dozen who circulated about her. Each of them had at one time been favored above all others—about half of them still basked in the solace of occasional sentimental revivals. Whenever one showed signs of dropping out through long neglect, she granted him a brief honeyed hour, which encouraged him to tag along for a year or so longer. Judy made these forays upon the helpless and defeated without malice, indeed half-unconscious that there was anything mischievous in what she did.

When a new man came to town everyone dropped out—dates were automatically canceled.

The helpless part of trying to do anything about it was that she did it all herself. She was not a girl who could be "won" in the kinetic sense—she was proof against cleverness, she was proof against charm; if any of these assailed her too strongly she would immediately resolve the affair to a physical basis, and under the magic of her physical splendor the strong as well as the brilliant played her game and not their own. She was entertained only by the gratification of her desires and by the direct exercise of her own charm. Perhaps from so much youthful love, so many youthful lovers, she had come, in self-defense, to nourish herself wholly from within.

Succeeding Dexter's first exhilaration came restlessness and dissatisfaction. The helpless ecstasy of losing himself in her was opiate rather than tonic. It was fortunate for his work during the winter that those moments of ecstasy came infrequently. Early in their acquaintance it had seemed for a while that there was a deep and spontaneous mutual attraction—that first August, for example—three days of long evenings on her dusky veranda, of strange wan kisses through the late afternoon, in shadowy alcoves or behind the protecting trellises of the garden arbors, of mornings when she was fresh as a dream and almost shy at meeting him in the clarity of the rising day. There was all the ecstasy of an engagement about it, sharpened by his realization that there was no engagement. It was during those three days that, for the first time, he had asked her to marry him. She said "maybe some day," she said "kiss me," she said "I'd like to marry you," she said "I love you"—she said—nothing.

The three days were interrupted by the arrival of a New York man who visited at her house for half September. To Dexter's agony, rumor engaged them. The man was the son of the president of a great trust company. But at the end of a month it was reported that Judy was yawning. At a dance one night she sat all evening in a motorboat with a local beau, while the New Yorker searched the club for her frantically. She told the local beau that she was bored with her visitor, and two days later he left. She was seen with him at the station, and it was reported that he looked very mournful indeed.

On this note the summer ended. Dexter was twenty-four, and he found himself increasingly in a position to do as he wished. He joined two clubs in the city and lived at one of them. Though he was by no means an integral part of the stag lines at these clubs, he managed to be on hand at dances where Judy Jones was likely to appear. He could have gone out socially as much as he liked—he was an eligible young man, now, and popular with downtown fathers. His confessed devotion to Judy Jones had rather solidified his position. But he had no social aspirations and rather despised the dancing men who were always on tap for the Thursday or Saturday parties and who filled in at dinners with the younger married set. Already he was playing with the idea of going east to New York. He wanted to take Judy Jones with him. No disillusion as to the world in which she had grown up could cure his illusion as to her desirability.

Remember that—for only in the light of it can what he did for her be understood.

Eighteen months after he first met Judy Jones he became engaged to another girl. Her name was Irene Scheerer, and her father was one of the men who had always believed in Dexter. Irene was light-haired and sweet and honorable, and a little stout, and she had two suitors whom she pleasantly relinquished when Dexter formally asked her to marry him.

Summer, fall, winter, spring, another summer, another fall—so much he had given of his active life to the incorrigible lips of Judy Jones. She had treated him with interest, with encouragement, with malice, with indifference, with contempt. She had inflicted on him the innumerable little slights and indignities possible in such a case—as if in revenge for having ever cared for him at all. She had beckoned him and yawned at him and beckoned him again and he had responded often with bitterness and narrowed eyes. She had brought him ecstatic happiness and intolerable agony of spirit. She had caused him untold inconvenience and not a little trouble. She had insulted him, and she had ridden over him, and she had played his interest in her against his interest in his work—for fun. She had done everything to him except to criticize him—this she had not done—it seemed to him only because it might have sullied the utter indifference she manifested and sincerely felt toward him.

When autumn had come and gone again it occurred to him that he could not have Judy Jones. He had to beat this into his mind but he convinced himself at last. He lay awake at night for a while and argued it over. He told himself the trouble and the pain she had caused him, he enumerated her glaring deficiencies as a wife. Then he said to himself that he loved her, and after a while he fell asleep. For a week, lest he imagined her husky voice over the telephone or her eyes opposite him at lunch, he worked hard and late, and at night he went to his office and plotted out his years.

At the end of a week he went to a dance and cut in on her once. For almost the first time since they had met he did not ask her to sit out with him or tell her that she was lovely. It hurt him that she did not miss these things—that was all. He was not jealous when he saw that there was a new man tonight. He had been hardened against jealousy long before.

He stayed late at the dance. He sat for an hour with Irene Scheerer and talked about books and about music. He knew very little about either. But he was beginning to be master of his own time now, and he had a rather priggish notion that he—the young and already fabulously successful Dexter Green—should know more about such things.

That was in October, when he was twenty-five. In January, Dexter and Irene became engaged. It was to be announced in June, and they were to be married three months later.

The Minnesota winter prolonged itself interminably, and it was almost May when the winds came soft and the snow ran down into Black Bear Lake at last. For the first time in over a year Dexter was enjoying a certain tranquillity of spirit. Judy Jones had been in Florida, and afterward in Hot Springs, and somewhere she had been engaged, and somewhere she had broken it off. At first, when Dexter had definitely given her up, it had made him sad that people still linked them together and asked for news of her, but when he began to be placed at dinner next to Irene Scheerer people didn't ask him about her anymore—they told him about her. He ceased to be an authority on her.

May at last. Dexter walked the streets at night when the darkness was damp as rain, wondering that so soon, with so little done, so much of ecstasy had gone from him. May one year back had been marked by Judy's poignant, unforgivable, yet forgiven turbulence—it had been one of those rare times when he fancied she had grown to care for him. That old penny's worth of happiness he had spent for this bushel of content. He knew that Irene would be no more than a curtain spread behind him, a hand moving among gleaming teacups, a voice calling to children . . . fire and loveliness were gone, the magic of nights and the wonder of the varying hours and seasons . . . slender lips, down-turning, dropping to his lips and bearing him up into a heaven of eyes . . . The thing was deep in him. He was too strong and alive for it to die lightly.

In the middle of May, when the weather balanced for a few days on the thin bridge that led to deep summer, he turned in one night at Irene's house. Their engagement was to be announced in a week now—no one would be surprised at it. And tonight they would sit together on the lounge at the University Club and look on for an hour at the dancers. It gave him a sense of solidity to go with her—she was so sturdily popular, so intensely "great."

He mounted the steps of the brownstone house and stepped inside.

"Irene," he called.

Mrs. Scheerer came out of the living room to meet him.

"Dexter," she said, "Irene's gone upstairs with a splitting headache. She wanted to go with you but I made her go to bed."

"Nothing serious, I—"

"Oh, no. She's going to play golf with you in the morning. You can spare her for just one night, can't you, Dexter?"

Her smile was kind. She and Dexter liked each other. In the living room he talked for a moment before he said good-night.

Returning to the University Club, where he had rooms, he stood in the doorway for a moment and watched the dancers. He leaned against the doorpost, nodded at a man or two—yawned.

"Hello, darling."

The familiar voice at his elbow startled him. Judy Jones had left a man and crossed the room to him—Judy Jones, a slender enameled doll in cloth of gold: gold in a band at her head, gold in two slipper points at her dress's hem. The fragile glow of her face seemed to blossom as she smiled at him. A breeze of warmth and light blew through the room. His hands in the pockets of his dinner jacket tightened spasmodically. He was filled with a sudden excitement.

"When did you get back?" he asked casually.

"Come here and I'll tell you about it."

She turned and he followed her. She had been away—he could have wept at the wonder of her return. She had passed through enchanted streets, doing things that were like provocative music. All mysterious happenings, all fresh and quickening hopes, had gone away with her, come back with her now.

She turned in the doorway.

"Have you a car here? If you haven't, I have."

"I have a coupe."

In then, with a rustle of golden cloth. He slammed the door. Into so many cars she had stepped—like this—like that—her back against the leather, so—her elbow resting on the door—waiting. She would have been soiled long since had there been anything to soil her—except herself—but this was her own self outpouring.

With an effort he forced himself to start the car and back into the street. This was nothing, he must remember. She had done this before, and he had put her behind him, as he would have crossed a bad account from his books.

He drove slowly downtown and, affecting abstraction, traversed the deserted streets of the business section, peopled here and there where a movie was giving out its crowd or where consumptive or pugilistic youth lounged in front of pool halls. The clink of glasses and the slap of hands on the bars issued from saloons, cloisters of glazed glass and dirty yellow light.

She was watching him closely and the silence was embarrassing, yet in this crisis he could find no casual word with which to profane the hour. At a convenient turning he began to zigzag back toward the University Club.

"Have you missed me?" she asked suddenly.

"Everybody missed you."

He wondered if she knew of Irene Scheerer. She had been back only a day—her absence had been almost contemporaneous with his engagement.

"What a remark!" Judy laughed sadly—without sadness. She looked at him searchingly. He became absorbed in the dashboard.

"You're handsomer than you used to be," she said thoughtfully. "Dexter, you have the most rememberable eyes."

He could have laughed at this, but he did not laugh. It was the sort of thing that was said to sophomores. Yet it stabbed at him.

"I'm awfully tired of everything, darling." She called everyone darling, endowing the endearment with careless, individual camaraderie. "I wish you'd marry me."

The directness of this confused him. He should have told her now that he was going to marry another girl, but he could not tell her. He could as easily have sworn that he had never loved her.

"I think we'd get along," she continued, on the same note, "unless probably you've forgotten me and fallen in love with another girl."

Her confidence was obviously enormous. She had said, in effect, that she found such a thing impossible to believe, that if it were true he had merely committed a childish indiscretion—and probably to show off. She would forgive him, because it was not a matter of any moment but rather something to be brushed aside lightly.

"Of course you could never love anybody but me," she continued, "I like the way you love me. Oh, Dexter, have you forgotten last year?"

"No, I haven't forgotten."

"Neither have I!"

Was she sincerely moved—or was she carried along by the wave of her own acting?

"I wish we could be like that again," she said, and he forced himself to answer:

"I don't think we can."

"I suppose not. . . . I hear you're giving Irene Scheerer a violent rush."

There was not the faintest emphasis on the name, yet Dexter was suddenly ashamed.

"Oh, take me home," cried Judy suddenly, "I don't want to go back to that idiotic dance—with those children."

Then, as he turned up the street that led to the residence district, Judy began to cry quietly to herself. He had never seen her cry before.

The dark street lightened, the dwellings of the rich loomed up around them, he stopped his coupe in front of the great white bulk of the Mortimer Joneses' house, somnolent, gorgeous, drenched with the splendor of the damp moonlight. Its solidity startled him. The strong walls, the steel of the girders, the breadth and beam and pomp of it were there only to bring out the contrast with the young beauty beside him. It was sturdy to accentuate her slightness—as if to show what a breeze could be generated by a butterfly's wing.

He sat perfectly quiet, his nerve in wild clamor, afraid that if he moved he would find her irresistibly in his arms. Two tears had rolled down her wet face and trembled on her upper lip.

"I'm more beautiful than anybody else," she said brokenly, "why can't I be happy?" Her moist eyes tore at his stability—her mouth turned slowly downward with an exquisite sadness: "I'd like to marry you if you'll have me, Dexter. I suppose you think I'm not worth having, but I'll be so beautiful for you, Dexter."

A million phrases of anger, pride, passion, hatred, tenderness fought on his lips. Then a perfect wave of emotion washed over him, carrying off with it a sediment of wisdom, of convention, of doubt, of honor. This was his girl who was speaking, his own, his beautiful, his pride.

"Won't you come in?" He heard her draw in her breath sharply.

Waiting.

"All right," his voice was trembling, "I'll come in."

V

It was strange that neither when it was over nor a long time afterward did he regret that night. Looking at it from the perspective of ten years, the fact that Judy's flare for him endured just one month seemed of little importance. Nor did it matter that by his yielding he subjected himself to a deeper agony in the end and gave serious hurt to Irene Scheerer and to Irene's parents, who had befriended him. There was nothing sufficiently pictorial about Irene's grief to stamp itself on his mind.

Dexter was at bottom hard-minded. The attitude of the city on his action was of no importance to him, not because he was going to leave the city, but because any outside attitude on the situation seemed superficial. He was completely indifferent to popular opinion. Nor, when he had seen that it was no use, that he did not possess in himself the power to move fundamentally or to hold Judy Jones, did he bear any malice toward her. He loved her, and he would love her until the day he was too old for loving—but he could not have her. So he tasted the deep pain that is reserved only for the strong, just as he had tasted for a little while the deep happiness.

Even the ultimate falsity of the grounds upon which Judy terminated the engagement, that she did not want to "take him away" from Irene—Judy, who had wanted nothing else—did not revolt him. He was beyond any revulsion or any amusement.

He went east in February with the intention of selling out his laundries and settling in New York—but the war came to America in March and changed his plans. He returned to the West, handed over the management of the business to his partner, and went into the first officers' training camp in late April. He was one of those young thousands who greeted the war with a certain amount of relief, welcoming the liberation from webs of tangled emotion.

VI

This story is not his biography, remember, although things creep into it which have nothing to do with those dreams he had when he was young. We are almost done with them and with him now. There is only one more incident to be related here, and it happens seven years farther on.

It took place in New York, where he had done well—so well that there were no barriers too high for him. He was thirty-two years old, and, except for one flying trip immediately after the war, he had not been west in seven years. A man named Devlin from Detroit came into his office to see him in a business way, and then and there this incident occurred, and closed out, so to speak, this particular side of his life.

"So you're from the Middle West," said the man Devlin with careless curiosity. "That's funny—I thought men like you were probably born and raised on Wall Street. You know—wife of one of my best friends in Detroit came from your city. I was an usher at the wedding."

Dexter waited with no apprehension of what was coming.

"Judy Simms," said Devlin with no particular interest. "Judy Jones she was once."

"Yes, I knew her." A dull impatience spread over him. He had heard, of course, that she was married—perhaps deliberately he had heard no more.

"Awfully nice girl," brooded Devlin meaninglessly, "I'm sort of sorry for her."

"Why?" Something in Dexter was alert, receptive, at once.

"Oh, Lud Simms has gone to pieces in a way. I don't mean he ill-uses her, but he drinks and runs around—"

"Doesn't she run around?"

"No. Stays at home with her kids."

"Oh."

"She's a little too old for him," said Devlin.

"Too old!" cried Dexter. "Why, man, she's only twenty-seven."

He was possessed with a wild notion of rushing out into the streets and taking a train to Detroit. He rose to his feet spasmodically.

"I guess you're busy," Devlin apologized quickly. "I didn't realize—"

"No, I'm not busy," said Dexter, steadying his voice. "I'm not busy at all. Not busy at all. Did you say she was—twenty-seven? No, I said she was twenty-seven."

"Yes, you did," agreed Devlin dryly.

"Go on, then. Go on."

"What do you mean?"

"About Judy Jones."

Devlin looked at him helplessly.

"Well, that's—I told you all there is to it. He treats her like the devil. Oh, they're not going to get divorced or anything. When he's particularly outrageous she forgives him. In fact, I'm inclined to think she loves him. She was a pretty girl when she first came to Detroit."

A pretty girl! The phrase struck Dexter as ludicrous.

"Isn't she—a pretty girl, anymore?"

"Oh, she's all right."

"Look here," said Dexter, sitting down suddenly. "I don't understand. You say she was a 'pretty girl' and now you say she's 'all right.' I don't understand what you mean—Judy Jones wasn't a pretty girl, at all. She was a great beauty. Why, I knew her, I knew her. She was—"

Devlin laughed pleasantly.

"I'm not trying to start a row," he said. "I think Judy's a nice girl and I like her. I can't understand how a man like Lud Simms could fall madly in love with her, but he did." Then he added: "Most of the women like her."

Dexter looked closely at Devlin, thinking wildly that there must be a reason for this, some insensitivity in the man or some private malice.

"Lots of women fade just like *that*," Devlin snapped his fingers. "You must have seen it happen. Perhaps I've forgotten how pretty she was at her wedding. I've seen her so much since then, you see. She has nice eyes."

A sort of dullness settled down upon Dexter. For the first time in his life he felt like getting very drunk. He knew that he was laughing loudly at something Devlin had said, but he did not know what it was or why it was funny. When, in a few minutes, Devlin went he lay down on his lounge and looked out the window at the New York skyline into which the sun was sinking in dull lovely shades of pink and gold.

He had thought that having nothing else to lose he was invulnerable at last—but he knew that he had just lost something more, as surely as if he had married Judy Jones and seen her fade away before his eyes.

The dream was gone. Something had been taken from him. In a sort of panic he pushed the palms of his hands into his eyes and tried to bring up a picture of the waters lapping on Sherry Island and the moonlit veranda, and gingham on the golf links and the dry sun and the gold color of her neck's soft down. And her mouth damp to his kisses and her eyes plaintive with melancholy and her freshness like new fine linen in the morning. Why, these things were no longer in the world! They had existed and they existed no longer.

For the first time in years the tears were streaming down his face. But they were for himself now. He did not care about mouth and eyes and moving hands. He wanted to care, and he could not care. For he had gone away and he could never go back anymore. The gates were closed, the sun was gone down, and there was no beauty but the gray beauty of steel that withstands all time. Even the grief he could have borne was left behind in the country of illusion, of youth, of the richness of life, where his winter dreams had flourished.

"Long ago," he said, "long ago, there was something in me, but now that thing is gone. Now that thing is gone, that thing is gone. I cannot cry. I cannot care. That thing will come back no more."

What are the "winter dreams" that unconsciously dictate to Dexter?

1. Why does Dexter find the spring dismal and the fall gorgeous and full of hope?

2. Why is Dexter offended that the golf links "lie in enforced fallowness" during the winter? (17)

3. How does wanting "the glittering things themselves," not just "association with glittering things and glittering people," keep Dexter from being "merely snobbish"? (21)

4. When he returns to the course and plays golf in a foursome with Mr. Hart, is it more important to Dexter to hide his past as a caddy or to "lessen the gap which lay between his present and his past"? (22)

5. When Dexter hears the piano music over the water, why is it a song that was popular five years earlier that "precipitated in him a sort of ecstasy"? (23–24)

6. What does Judy Jones have to do with Dexter's winter dreams?

7. At the end of the story, why does Dexter suddenly see his winter dreams as illusion? Why can he no longer treasure even his memories of Judy Jones?

Why do Judy Jones's casual whims repeatedly give new direction to Dexter's life?

1. Why would Dexter rather quit his job than caddy for Judy Jones? What is the "strong emotional shock" he experiences? (20)

2. How can Judy's smile be simultaneously "blatantly artificial" and "convincing"? (19)

3. Why is Judy Jones always referred to by both her first and last names?

4. Why does Judy Jones flee from the man who says she's his ideal?

5. How does Judy Jones create "want by holding back nothing at all"? (27)

6. Is Dexter better than the other men who love Judy Jones?

7. Why doesn't Dexter regret his brief reunion with Judy Jones or the pain he causes Irene Scheerer and her parents?

Why is Dexter devastated when he hears what became of Judy Jones?

1. Why does Devlin's account of the former Judy Jones finally kill Dexter's dream?

2. Why does Dexter feel "a dull impatience" when Devlin mentions Judy Jones? (35) Why doesn't he want to know what's become of her?

3. Why does listening to Devlin make Dexter feel that "he had just lost something more, as surely as if he had married Judy Jones and seen her fade away before his eyes"? (37)

4. Why are we told that Dexter "tasted the deep pain that is reserved only for the strong, just as he had tasted for a little while the deep happiness"? (35)

5. Why does the narrator tell us that "this story is not his [Dexter's] biography, remember"? (35) What is it, if not a biography?

6. What has Dexter lost at the end of the story? What has Judy Jones lost?

7. Was Dexter's disillusionment inevitable?

The Great Gatsby

Interpretive Questions
for Discussion

♣☙♣

*The following questions suggest a wide range of possibilities for interpretation.
Some of the questions are keyed to the passages for close reading (pp. 51–83), and careful reading
of these passages either before or during discussion allows you to consider the
various possible answers to the discussion questions more thoroughly.*

*Keep in mind that everyone, including the discussion leader, is an equal partner in
interpretation and understanding. Do not expect a teacher or leader to provide answers to
the questions that follow; instead, listen to individual ideas during discussion, test
the validity of your own thoughts, and learn from the group.*

These questions have been organized for discussion of the novel as a whole or by chapter. All quotations are from the Scribner Paperback Fiction edition of The Great Gatsby *(first edition 1995).*

In what sense is Gatsby "great"?

1. At the beginning of the novel, why does Nick say that Gatsby "represented everything for which I have an unaffected scorn"? Why does Nick then say that only Gatsby was "exempt" from his feeling that he "wanted no more riotous excursions with privileged glimpses into the human heart"?

2. Why does Nick say of Gatsby, "If personality is an unbroken series of successful gestures, then there was something gorgeous about him"?

3. What is Gatsby's "romantic readiness"?

4. What does Nick mean when he says that "Gatsby turned out all right at the end"?

5. Why does Gatsby fail in his effort to make real the world he imagines?

6. What does Nick think "preyed on" Gatsby?

Who, or what, is primarily responsible for Gatsby's fate?

Passage 11

1. Is Gatsby's feeling for Daisy idealistic or self-indulgent? Why does Nick compare Gatsby's pursuit of Daisy to "the following of a grail"?

Passage 10

2. Why doesn't Daisy hold to her decision to leave Tom for Gatsby?

3. Why does Daisy agree to meet Gatsby secretly and otherwise encourage his love for her?

4. Are we meant to disapprove of Gatsby's business dealings and his intense pursuit of wealth?

5. Why are we told that, after the accident, Daisy and Tom look neither happy nor unhappy, but seem to be "conspiring together" when Nick sees them through the window? Why does Tom tell Wilson that Gatsby killed Myrtle, and let Wilson know where to find Gatsby?

6. Why does Tom break off his explanation "defiantly" when Nick confronts him after Gatsby's funeral? Why does Nick feel "suddenly as though I were talking to a child"?

Why does Nick alternately admire and disapprove of Gatsby and the life he has led?

1. In the end, is Nick still reserving his judgment of Gatsby, or has he come to some conclusion about him?

2. Is Nick changed by his experience with Gatsby?

3. Why does Nick say that Gatsby was about "the service of a vast, vulgar and meretricious beauty"? Does Nick see Gatsby's faithfulness to his conception of himself as admirable, pitiable, or something else?

4. Why does Nick tell Gatsby, "They're a rotten crowd. . . . You're worth the whole damn bunch put together"? Why does he go on to say, "I've always been glad I said that. It was the only compliment I ever gave him, because I disapproved of him from beginning to end"?

5. Why is it so important to Nick that people attend Gatsby's funeral? Why is Nick the only main character who attends?

6. At the end of the novel, why does Nick say "we" in "we beat on, boats against the current, borne back ceaselessly into the past"? Is he suggesting we are all like Gatsby, or is he suggesting something else?

Passage 15

Chapter 1

1. What is Nick afraid of missing if he forgets that "a sense of the fundamental decencies is parcelled out unequally at birth"? Why does he say that reserving judgments "is a matter of infinite hope"?

2. Why is Tom so taken with racist theories of white superiority? Why does he want to believe that these theories are scientific and accurate?

3. Are Daisy's voice and manner natural to her, or is she acting? Why are so many men so attracted to her?

4. Why does Daisy tell Nick "the best thing a girl can be in this world" is a "beautiful little fool"? Why does Nick feel that Daisy's words are insincere?

5. Why does Jordan seem "discontented" to Nick? Why does she want to eavesdrop on Tom's phone conversation?

6. What do Tom and Daisy want from Nick?

7. Why is Nick "confused and a little disgusted" as he drives away from Tom and Daisy's house?

Passage 1   8. What is it about Gatsby's first appearance that keeps Nick from approaching him?

Chapter 2

Passage 2   1. Why does Nick describe the valley of ashes as "fantastic" and "grotesque"? Why does he say that Doctor T. J. Eckleburg's eyes "brood on over the solemn dumping ground"?

2. Why does Fitzgerald have Myrtle live above a garage on "the edge of the wasteland"?

Passage 3   3. Why is Myrtle attracted to Tom? Why does she put on airs when they get to the New York apartment?

4. Does Wilson suspect that Myrtle and Tom are having an affair?

5. Why does Tom break Myrtle's nose when she keeps saying Daisy's name?

6. How do the rumors about Gatsby contribute to his image and reputation?

Chapter 3

1. Why doesn't Nick realize who Gatsby is when the two men meet at Gatsby's party?   *Passage 5*

2. Why does Gatsby spend most of his party alone, instead of mingling with the guests? Why doesn't he seem to mind that so many of the people there were not invited?

3. Why does the party end with the car crash involving the owl-eyed man?

4. Why does Nick continue to associate with Jordan despite thinking she is "incurably dishonest"?

5. What does Jordan mean when she tells Nick, "I hate careless people. That's why I like you"?   *Passage 6*

6. Is Nick as honest as he says he is?   *Passage 6*

Chapter 4

1. Why does Nick list all the people who attended Gatsby's parties that summer?

2. How is "knowing nothing whatever about him" a "subtle tribute" paid to Gatsby by his guests?

3. Why does Gatsby tell Nick the story of his life after asking for Nick's opinion of him?

4. When he crosses the bridge to the city with Gatsby, why does Nick say that now "even Gatsby could happen, without any particular wonder"?

5. Why does Wolfshiem draw Nick's attention to his cuff buttons and point out that they are actually human molars?

6. Why does Gatsby tell Nick "coolly," but after a hesitation, that Wolfshiem fixed the 1919 World Series?

7. Why does Gatsby have Jordan ask Nick if he'll invite Daisy to his house, instead of asking Nick himself?

8. Does Jordan believe that Daisy was in love with Gatsby when she married Tom? What is Jordan's attitude toward Daisy's past?

Chapter 5

1. Why does Gatsby call Nick "old sport"?

2. Why does Gatsby insist he doesn't want to put Nick to any trouble by having him invite Daisy over? Why does Gatsby want his first meeting with Daisy to be at Nick's house?

3. Why does Gatsby try, and fail, to act nonchalant when he sees Daisy again? Why does he run around the house in order to knock on the front door and appear to arrive after Daisy?

4. What is Daisy feeling during the meeting with Gatsby at Nick's house?

5. Why does Gatsby want Nick to come along while he shows off his house to Daisy?

6. Why does Daisy bury her face in Gatsby's beautiful shirts and cry?

7. Why has the "colossal significance" of the green light at the end of Daisy's dock "vanished forever" once Gatsby has met Daisy again?

Chapter 6

1. Why does Nick feel it is important to give a biography of James Gatz/ Jay Gatsby at this point to "clear this set of misconceptions away," even though he learned the facts much later?   *Passage 8*

2. Why does James Gatz change his name to Jay Gatsby at age seventeen? Why does Nick say, "I suppose he'd had the name ready for a long time, even then"?   *Passage 8*

3. Why does Gatsby so desperately want to see more of Tom? Why does he try to join the horse-riding party for supper, even after Mr. Sloane and the others have made it clear they don't want him?

4. Why is the atmosphere at Gatsby's completely changed for Nick the first time Tom and Daisy attend a party there? Why does Gatsby refer to Tom all evening as "the polo player"?

5. What does Gatsby mean when he says, "I feel far away from her. It's hard to make her understand"?

6. Why is Gatsby so sure that it is possible to repeat the past? What is Nick reminded of as Gatsby talks about the past? What does he want to say to Gatsby, and why can't he manage to say it?

Chapter 7

1. Why does Gatsby say that Daisy's voice is "full of money"? Why does Nick think "that was it"?

2. Why does Tom insist on driving Gatsby's car, despite Gatsby's distaste for the idea? Why does Tom call Gatsby's car a "circus wagon"?

3. Why is Gatsby "content" once Tom has brought the affair with Daisy "out in the open at last"?

4. Why is Gatsby so upset when Daisy tells him that she did love Tom "once—but I loved you too"?   *Passage 10*

5. Why does Daisy draw "further and further into herself" as Gatsby tries to defend himself against Tom's accusations? Why are Daisy's "intentions" and "courage" now "definitely gone"?

6. After Tom and Gatsby's argument, why does Nick suddenly realize that it's his thirtieth birthday?

7. Why does Gatsby admit to Nick that Daisy was driving the car when Myrtle was killed?

8. Why doesn't Nick tell Gatsby that he saw Daisy and Tom "conspiring together"?

Chapter 8

1. Why does Gatsby still wait for Daisy even though Nick senses that "'Jay Gatsby' had broken up like glass against Tom's hard malice and the long secret extravaganza was played out"?

Passage 11

2. Why doesn't Gatsby feel guilty for wooing Daisy under false pretenses? Why does he suddenly find that he has "committed himself to the following of a grail"?

3. What does Gatsby mean when he says of Daisy's feelings for Tom, "In any case, . . . it was just personal"?

4. Why doesn't Nick want to leave Gatsby the morning after the accident?

5. Why do Nick and Jordan have such a tense conversation? Why is Nick "annoyed" that Jordan has left the Buchanans' house?

Passage 12

6. How are the circumstances and setting of Gatsby's death consistent with his life and personality?

Chapter 9

1. Why is it so important to Nick that he "get somebody" for Gatsby?

2. Why are Gatsby's father, Nick, and the owl-eyed man the only named characters who come to the funeral?

   Passage 14

3. What is Nick thinking as he repeats, "It just shows you," when Gatsby's father shows him Gatsby's early schedule for self-improvement?

4. Why does the owl-eyed man say, "The poor son-of-a-bitch," after the funeral? Why is he given the last word at the funeral?

   Passage 14

5. Are we supposed to agree with Jordan that Nick isn't straightforward or honest, or with Nick when he says he's "five years too old to lie to myself and call it honor"?

6. At the end of the novel, why does Nick return to Gatsby's abandoned house and rub out the obscene word on the steps?

The Great Gatsby

Passages and Questions
for Close Reading

*The questions that follow these passages encourage close reading and, taken together,
constitute a rigorous study of literary themes, techniques, and terms. All readers will benefit from
the challenges these questions pose, and students in honors courses or courses qualifying
for college credit will find these questions useful for exam preparation.*

Passage 1

Already it was deep summer on roadhouse roofs and in front of wayside garages where new red gas-pumps sat out in pools of light, and when I reached my estate at West Egg I ran the car under its shed and sat for a while on an abandoned grass roller in the yard. The wind had blown off, leaving a loud bright night with wings beating in the trees and a persistent organ sound as the full bellows of the earth blew the frogs full of life. The silhouette of a moving cat wavered across the moonlight and turning my head to watch it I saw that I was not alone—fifty feet away a figure had emerged from the shadow of my neighbor's mansion and was standing with his hands in his pockets regarding the silver pepper of the stars. Something in his leisurely movements and the secure position of his feet upon the lawn suggested that it was Mr. Gatsby himself, come out to determine what share was his of our local heavens.

I decided to call to him. Miss Baker had mentioned him at dinner, and that would do for an introduction. But I didn't call to him for he gave a sudden intimation that he was content to be alone—he stretched out his arms toward the dark water in a curious way, and far as I was from him I could have sworn he was trembling. Involuntarily I glanced seaward—and distinguished nothing except a single green light, minute and far away, that might have been the end of a dock. When I looked once more for Gatsby he had vanished, and I was alone again in the unquiet darkness.

1. What literary technique is Fitzgerald using when Nick refers to the "silver pepper of the stars"?

2. What impression of Gatsby is suggested by the phrase "come out to determine what share was his of our local heavens"?

3. Rather than "my neighbor's mansion," why does the narrator tell us that the figure emerged from "the shadow" of it?

4. What features of the landscape convey symbolic meaning? What behaviors or actions on the part of Nick and Gatsby are symbolic?

5. What are the literal and figurative meanings of "unquiet darkness"?

Passage 2

About half way between West Egg and New York the motor-road hastily joins the railroad and runs beside it for a quarter of a mile so as to shrink away from a certain desolate area of land. This is a valley of ashes—a fantastic farm where ashes grow like wheat into ridges and hills and grotesque gardens, where ashes take the forms of houses and chimneys and rising smoke and finally, with a transcendent effort, of men who move dimly and already crumbling through the powdery air. Occasionally a line of grey cars crawls along an invisible track, gives out a ghastly creak and comes to rest, and immediately the ash-grey men swarm up with leaden spades and stir up an impenetrable cloud which screens their obscure operations from your sight.

But above the grey land and the spasms of bleak dust which drift endlessly over it, you perceive, after a moment, the eyes of Doctor T. J. Eckleburg are blue and gigantic—their retinas are one yard high. They look out of no face but, instead, from a pair of enormous yellow spectacles which pass over a nonexistent nose. Evidently some wild wag of an oculist set them there to fatten his practice in the borough of Queens and then sank down himself into eternal blindness or forgot them and moved away. But his eyes, dimmed a little by many paintless days under sun and rain, brood on over the solemn dumping ground.

The valley of ashes is bounded on one side by a small foul river, and when the drawbridge is up to let barges through, the passengers on waiting trains can stare at the dismal scene for as long as half an hour. There is always a halt there of at least a minute and it was because of this that I first met Tom Buchanan's mistress.

∽

1. How are personification and hyperbole used in this passage to describe the valley of ashes? What is the effect?

2. Of the various forms that the ashes take, why is it only "with a transcendent effort" that they take the form of men?

3. Why does the narrator address the reader in the second person when describing the valley of ashes?

4. Why is the billboard not introduced as such, but as "the eyes of Dr. T. J. Eckleburg"?

5. What words in this passage emphasize the desolation of the valley of ashes?

Passage 3

The sister, Catherine, was a slender, worldly girl of about thirty with a solid sticky bob of red hair and a complexion powdered milky white. Her eyebrows had been plucked and then drawn on again at a more rakish angle but the efforts of nature toward the restoration of the old alignment gave a blurred air to her face. When she moved about there was an incessant clicking as innumerable pottery bracelets jingled up and down upon her arms. She came in with such a proprietary haste and looked around so possessively at the furniture that I wondered if she lived here. But when I asked her she laughed immoderately, repeated my question aloud and told me she lived with a girl friend at a hotel.

Mr. McKee was a pale feminine man from the flat below. He had just shaved for there was a white spot of lather on his cheekbone and he was most respectful in his greeting to everyone in the room. He informed me that he was in the "artistic game" and I gathered later that he was a photographer and had made the dim enlargement of Mrs. Wilson's mother which hovered like an ectoplasm on the wall. His wife was shrill, languid, handsome and horrible. She told me with pride that her husband had photographed her a hundred and twenty-seven times since they had been married.

Mrs. Wilson had changed her costume some time before and was now attired in an elaborate afternoon dress of cream colored chiffon which gave out a continual rustle as she swept about the room. With the influence of the dress her personality had also undergone a change. The intense vitality that had been so remarkable in the garage was converted into impressive hauteur. Her laughter, her gestures, her assertions became more violently affected moment by moment and as she expanded the room grew smaller around her until she seemed to be revolving on a noisy, creaking pivot through the smoky air.

"My dear," she told her sister in a high mincing shout, "most of these fellas will cheat you every time. All they think of is money. I had a woman up here last week to look at my feet and when she gave me the bill you'd of thought she had my appendicitus out."

"What was the name of the woman?" asked Mrs. McKee.

"Mrs. Eberhardt. She goes around looking at people's feet in their own homes."

"I like your dress," remarked Mrs. McKee. "I think it's adorable."

Mrs. Wilson rejected the compliment by raising her eyebrow in disdain.

"It's just a crazy old thing," she said. "I just slip it on sometimes when I don't care what I look like."

"But it looks wonderful on you, if you know what I mean," pursued Mrs. McKee. "If Chester could only get you in that pose I think he could make something of it."

We all looked in silence at Mrs. Wilson who removed a strand of hair from over her eyes and looked back at us with a brilliant smile. Mr. McKee regarded her intently with his head on one side and then moved his hand back and forth slowly in front of his face.

"I should change the light," he said after a moment. "I'd like to bring out the modelling of the features. And I'd try to get hold of all the back hair."

1. What is meant by Nick's observation about Myrtle that "as she expanded the room grew smaller around her until she seemed to be revolving on a noisy, creaking pivot through the smoky air"?

2. In what specific ways are Myrtle and Mrs. McKee affecting upper-class attitudes?

3. What does the simile "like an ectoplasm" suggest about Nick's impression of the photograph of Myrtle's mother on the wall?

4. What does this scene suggest about the nature of Catherine and Myrtle's relationship?

5. At the end of this passage, how do Myrtle's pose and Mr. McKee's comments on it emphasize the staginess of the scene?

Passage 4

There was music from my neighbor's house through the summer nights. In his blue gardens men and girls came and went like moths among the whisperings and the champagne and the stars. At high tide in the afternoon I watched his guests diving from the tower of his raft or taking the sun on the hot sand of his beach while his two motor boats slit the waters of the Sound, drawing aquaplanes over cataracts of foam. On week-ends his Rolls-Royce became an omnibus, bearing parties to and from the city, between nine in the morning and long past midnight, while his station wagon scampered like a brisk yellow bug to meet all trains. And on Mondays eight servants including an extra gardener toiled all day with mops and scrubbing-brushes and hammers and garden shears, repairing the ravages of the night before.

Every Friday five crates of oranges and lemons arrived from a fruiterer in New York—every Monday these same oranges and lemons left his back door in a pyramid of pulpless halves. There was a machine in the kitchen which could extract the juice of two hundred oranges in half an hour, if a little button was pressed two hundred times by a butler's thumb.

At least once a fortnight a corps of caterers came down with several hundred feet of canvas and enough colored lights to make a Christmas tree of Gatsby's enormous garden. On buffet tables, garnished with glistening hors d'oeuvre, spiced baked hams crowded against salads of harlequin designs and pastry pigs and turkeys bewitched to a dark gold. In the main hall a bar with a real brass rail was set up, and stocked with gins and liquors and with cordials so long forgotten that most of his female guests were too young to know one from another.

By seven o'clock the orchestra has arrived—no thin five piece affair but a whole pit full of oboes and trombones and saxophones and viols and cornets and piccolos and low and high drums. The last swimmers have come in from the beach now and are dressing upstairs; the cars from New York are parked five deep in the drive, and already the halls and salons and verandas are gaudy with primary colors and hair shorn in strange new ways and shawls beyond the dreams of Castile. The bar is in full swing and floating rounds of cocktails permeate the garden outside until the air is alive with chatter and laughter and casual innuendo and introductions forgotten on the spot and enthusiastic meetings between women who never knew each other's names.

The lights grow brighter as the earth lurches away from the sun and now the orchestra is playing yellow cocktail music and the opera of voices pitches a key higher. Laughter is easier, minute by minute, spilled with prodigality, tipped out at a cheerful word. The groups change more swiftly, swell with new arrivals, dissolve and form in the same breath—already there are wanderers, confident girls who weave here and there among the stouter and more stable, become for a sharp, joyous moment the center of a group and then excited with triumph glide on through the sea-change of faces and voices and color under the constantly changing light.

Suddenly one of these gypsies in trembling opal seizes a cocktail out of the air, dumps it down for courage and moving her hands like Frisco dances out alone on the canvas platform. A momentary hush; the orchestra leader varies his rhythm obligingly for her and there is a burst of chatter as the erroneous news goes around that she is Gilda Gray's understudy from the "Follies." The party has begun.

1. Why does Fitzgerald shift tense when describing the preparations and first arrivals for one of Gatsby's parties?

2. What is the effect of cataloguing the ingredients of a Gatsby party?

3. What literary technique is Fitzgerald using with the phrase "yellow cocktail music"? What effect does it have on this passage?

4. What do Gatsby's party and its music have in common?

Passage 5

I was still with Jordan Baker. We were sitting at a table with a man of about my age and a rowdy little girl who gave way upon the slightest provocation to uncontrollable laughter. I was enjoying myself now. I had taken two finger bowls of champagne and the scene had changed before my eyes into something significant, elemental and profound.

At a lull in the entertainment the man looked at me and smiled.

"Your face is familiar," he said politely. "Weren't you in the Third Division during the war?"

"Why, yes. I was in the Ninth Machine-Gun Battalion."

"I was in the Seventh Infantry until June nineteen-eighteen. I knew I'd seen you somewhere before."

We talked for a moment about some wet, grey little villages in France. Evidently he lived in this vicinity for he told me that he had just bought a hydroplane and was going to try it out in the morning.

"Want to go with me, old sport? Just near the shore along the Sound."

"What time?"

"Any time that suits you best."

It was on the tip of my tongue to ask his name when Jordan looked around and smiled.

"Having a gay time now?" she inquired.

"Much better." I turned again to my new acquaintance. "This is an unusual party for me. I haven't even seen the host. I live over there—" I waved my hand at the invisible hedge in the distance, "and this man Gatsby sent over his chauffeur with an invitation."

For a moment he looked at me as if he failed to understand.

"I'm Gatsby," he said suddenly.

"What!" I exclaimed. "Oh, I beg your pardon."

"I thought you knew, old sport. I'm afraid I'm not a very good host."

He smiled understandingly—much more than understandingly. It was one of those rare smiles with a quality of eternal reassurance in it, that you may come across four or five times in life. It faced—or seemed to face—the whole external world for an instant, and then concentrated on *you* with an irresistible prejudice in your favor. It understood you just so far as you wanted to be understood, believed in you as you would like to believe in yourself and assured you that it had precisely the impression of you that, at your best, you hoped to convey. Precisely at that point it vanished—and I was looking at an elegant young rough-neck, a year or two over thirty, whose elaborate formality of speech just missed being absurd. Some time before he introduced himself I'd got a strong impression that he was picking his words with care.

   Almost at the moment when Mr. Gatsby identified himself a butler hurried toward him with the information that Chicago was calling him on the wire. He excused himself with a small bow that included each of us in turn.

   "If you want anything just ask for it, old sport," he urged me. "Excuse me. I will rejoin you later."

1. What is Nick's tone when he observes that "the scene had changed before my eyes into something significant, elemental and profound"?

2. What are the connotations of the expression "old sport"? What does the expression accomplish or fail to accomplish?

3. When Gatsby assumes that Nick knows him and then apologizes to Nick for not being a very good host, what are we to understand about Gatsby's image of himself?

4. What is the effect of the qualification "or seemed to face" when Nick is describing Gatsby's smile?

5. When Gatsby's smile vanishes, how does Nick's impression of him change?

Passage 6

It made no difference to me. Dishonesty in a woman is a thing you never blame deeply—I was casually sorry, and then I forgot. It was on that same house party that we had a curious conversation about driving a car. It started because she passed so close to some workmen that our fender flicked a button on one man's coat.

"You're a rotten driver," I protested. "Either you ought to be more careful or you oughtn't to drive at all."

"I am careful."

"No, you're not."

"Well, other people are," she said lightly.

"What's that got to do with it?"

"They'll keep out of my way," she insisted. "It takes two to make an accident."

"Suppose you met somebody just as careless as yourself."

"I hope I never will," she answered. "I hate careless people. That's why I like you."

Her grey sun-strained eyes stared straight ahead, but she had deliberately shifted our relations, and for a moment I thought I loved her. But I am slow thinking and full of interior rules that act as brakes on my desires, and I knew that first I had to get myself definitely out of that tangle back home. I'd been writing letters once a week and signing them "Love, Nick," and all I could think of was how, when that certain girl played tennis, a faint mustache of perspiration appeared on her upper lip. Nevertheless there was a vague understanding that had to be tactfully broken off before I was free.

Everyone suspects himself of at least one of the cardinal virtues, and this is mine: I am one of the few honest people that I have ever known.

1. What is the larger significance of Nick and Jordan's conversation about driving, and what details in the passage make this evident?

2. What literary technique is Fitzgerald employing when Nick speaks of "interior rules that act as brakes on my desires"?

3. Why does Nick believe that his conversation with Jordan had "shifted [their] relations"?

4. What is the connotation of the word *suspects* as the narrator uses it in "Everyone suspects himself of at least one of the cardinal virtues"?

5. Can Nick as a narrator be objective about himself? Do you trust him? Is he reliable? Why or why not?

Passage 7

Outside the wind was loud and there was a faint flow of thunder along the Sound. All the lights were going on in West Egg now; the electric trains, men-carrying, were plunging home through the rain from New York. It was the hour of a profound human change and excitement was generating on the air.

> One thing's sure and nothing's surer
> The rich get richer and the poor get—children.
>> In the meantime,
>> In between time——

As I went over to say goodbye I saw that the expression of bewilderment had come back into Gatsby's face, as though a faint doubt had occurred to him as to the quality of his present happiness. Almost five years! There must have been moments even that afternoon when Daisy tumbled short of his dreams—not through her own fault but because of the colossal vitality of his illusion. It had gone beyond her, beyond everything. He had thrown himself into it with a creative passion, adding to it all the time, decking it out with every bright feather that drifted his way. No amount of fire or freshness can challenge what a man will store up in his ghostly heart.

As I watched him he adjusted himself a little, visibly. His hand took hold of hers and as she said something low in his ear he turned toward her with a rush of emotion. I think that voice held him most with its fluctuating, feverish warmth because it couldn't be over-dreamed—that voice was a deathless song.

They had forgotten me but Daisy glanced up and held out her hand; Gatsby didn't know me now at all. I looked once more at them and they looked back at me, remotely, possessed by intense life. Then I went out of the room and down the marble steps into the rain, leaving them there together.

1. What is the "profound human change" to which Nick is referring?

2. What is Nick's attitude toward the "colossal vitality of his [Gatsby's] illusion"? How does the language that Nick uses reveal this attitude?

3. What does Nick's characterization of Daisy's voice as "a deathless song" suggest about his understanding of Gatsby and Daisy's relationship?

4. What is the effect of setting this scene indoors while it is dark and stormy outside?

5. How do the lyrics Fitzgerald quotes affect the scene's emotional tone?

Passage 8

James Gatz—that was really, or at least legally, his name. He had changed it at the age of seventeen and at the specific moment that witnessed the beginning of his career—when he saw Dan Cody's yacht drop anchor over the most insidious flat on Lake Superior. It was James Gatz who had been loafing along the beach that afternoon in a torn green jersey and a pair of canvas pants, but it was already Jay Gatsby who borrowed a row-boat, pulled out to the *Tuolomee* and informed Cody that a wind might catch him and break him up in half an hour.

I suppose he'd had the name ready for a long time, even then. His parents were shiftless and unsuccessful farm people—his imagination had never really accepted them as his parents at all. The truth was that Jay Gatsby, of West Egg, Long Island, sprang from his Platonic conception of himself. He was a son of God—a phrase which, if it means anything, means just that—and he must be about His Father's Business, the service of a vast, vulgar and meretricious beauty. So he invented just the sort of Jay Gatsby that a seventeen year old boy would be likely to invent, and to this conception he was faithful to the end.

For over a year he had been beating his way along the south shore of Lake Superior as a clam digger and a salmon fisher or in any other capacity that brought him food and bed. His brown, hardening body lived naturally through the half fierce, half lazy work of the bracing days. He knew women early and since they spoiled him he became contemptuous of them, of young virgins because they were ignorant, of the others because they were hysterical about things which in his overwhelming self-absorption he took for granted.

But his heart was in a constant, turbulent riot. The most grotesque and fantastic conceits haunted him in his bed at night. A universe of ineffable gaudiness spun itself out in his brain while the clock ticked on the wash-stand and the moon soaked with wet light his tangled clothes upon the floor. Each night he added to the pattern of his fancies until drowsiness closed down upon some vivid scene with an oblivious embrace. For a while these reveries provided an outlet for his imagination; they were a satisfactory hint of the unreality of reality, a promise that the rock of the world was founded securely on a fairy's wing.

1. What difference does Nick imply between "really" and "legally" when he says that James Gatz was "really, or at least legally" Gatsby's name?

2. What does it mean for Jay Gatsby to have "spr[u]ng from his Platonic conception of himself" and to be "a son of God"?

3. What is Nick's tone when he calls Gatsby a "son of God" and says that Gatsby "must be about His Father's Business, the service of a vast, vulgar and meretricious beauty"?

4. What is meant by "the unreality of reality, a promise that the rock of the world was founded securely on a fairy's wing"? How are Gatsby's dreams initially a "satisfactory hint" of this?

5. How do the connotations of the language in this passage express a contrast between the world in which Gatsby lives and the one he imagines?

Passage 9

I stayed late that night. Gatsby asked me to wait until he was free and I lingered in the garden until the inevitable swimming party had run up, chilled and exalted, from the black beach, until the lights were extinguished in the guest rooms over-head. When he came down the steps at last the tanned skin was drawn unusually tight on his face, and his eyes were bright and tired.

"She didn't like it," he said immediately.

"Of course she did."

"She didn't like it," he insisted. "She didn't have a good time."

He was silent and I guessed at his unutterable depression.

"I feel far away from her," he said. "It's hard to make her understand."

"You mean about the dance?"

"The dance?" He dismissed all the dances he had given with a snap of his fin-gers. "Old sport, the dance is unimportant."

He wanted nothing less of Daisy than that she should go to Tom and say: "I never loved you." After she had obliterated three years with that sentence they could decide upon the more practical measures to be taken. One of them was that, after she was free, they were to go back to Louisville and be married from her house—just as if it were five years ago.

"And she doesn't understand," he said despairingly. "She used to be able to understand. We'd sit for hours——"

He broke off and began to walk up and down a desolate path of fruit rinds and discarded favors and crushed flowers.

"I wouldn't ask too much of her," I ventured. "You can't repeat the past."

"Can't repeat the past?" he cried incredulously. "Why of course you can!"

He looked around him wildly, as if the past were lurking here in the shadow of his house, just out of reach of his hand.

"I'm going to fix everything just the way it was before," he said, nodding determinedly. "She'll see."

He talked a lot about the past and I gathered that he wanted to recover some-thing, some idea of himself perhaps, that had gone into loving Daisy. His life had been confused and disordered since then, but if he could once return to a certain starting place and go over it all slowly, he could find out what that thing was. . . .

. . . One autumn night, five years before, they had been walking down the street when the leaves were falling, and they came to a place where there were no trees and the sidewalk was white with moonlight. They stopped here and turned toward each other. Now it was a cool night with that mysterious excitement in it which comes at the two changes of the year. The quiet lights in the houses were humming out into the darkness and there was a stir and bustle among the stars. Out of the corner of his eye Gatsby saw that the blocks of the sidewalk really formed a ladder and mounted to a secret place above the trees—he could climb to it, if he climbed alone, and once there he could suck on the pap of life, gulp down the incomparable milk of wonder.

His heart beat faster and faster as Daisy's white face came up to his own. He knew that when he kissed this girl, and forever wed his unutterable visions to her perishable breath, his mind would never romp again like the mind of God. So he waited, listening for a moment longer to the tuning fork that had been struck upon a star. Then he kissed her. At his lips' touch she blossomed for him like a flower and the incarnation was complete.

Through all he said, even through his appalling sentimentality, I was reminded of something—an elusive rhythm, a fragment of lost words, that I had heard somewhere a long time ago. For a moment a phrase tried to take shape in my mouth and my lips parted like a dumb man's, as though there was more struggling upon them than a wisp of startled air. But they made no sound and what I had almost remembered was uncommunicable forever.

1. How does Nick's description of the scene reflect Gatsby's mood?

2. What symbols does Fitzgerald use to convey the meaning and importance of Daisy in Gatsby's life?

3. What, specifically, do the ellipses in this passage separate?

4. How does Nick's reference to Gatsby's "appalling sentimentality" undermine the rhetoric of the preceding two paragraphs?

5. What is the collective effect of the words *elusive, fragment, dumb, struggling, wisp,* and *startled* in the last paragraph? How do these words help Fitzgerald communicate his idea?

Passage 10

"I've got something to tell *you,* old sport,—" began Gatsby. But Daisy guessed at his intention.

"Please don't!" she interrupted helplessly. "Please let's all go home. Why don't we all go home?"

"That's a good idea." I got up. "Come on, Tom. Nobody wants a drink."

"I want to know what Mr. Gatsby has to tell me."

"Your wife doesn't love you," said Gatsby quietly. "She's never loved you. She loves me."

"You must be crazy!" exclaimed Tom automatically.

Gatsby sprang to his feet, vivid with excitement.

"She never loved you, do you hear?" he cried. "She only married you because I was poor and she was tired of waiting for me. It was a terrible mistake, but in her heart she never loved anyone except me!"

At this point Jordan and I tried to go but Tom and Gatsby insisted with competitive firmness that we remain—as though neither of them had anything to conceal and it would be a privilege to partake vicariously of their emotions.

"Sit down Daisy." Tom's voice groped unsuccessfully for the paternal note. "What's been going on? I want to hear all about it."

"I told you what's been going on," said Gatsby. "Going on for five years—and you didn't know."

Tom turned to Daisy sharply.

"You've been seeing this fellow for five years?"

"Not seeing," said Gatsby. "No, we couldn't meet. But both of us loved each other all that time, old sport, and you didn't know. I used to laugh sometimes—" but there was no laughter in his eyes, "to think that you didn't know."

"Oh—that's all." Tom tapped his thick fingers together like a clergyman and leaned back in his chair.

"You're crazy!" he exploded. "I can't speak about what happened five years ago because I didn't know Daisy then—and I'll be damned if I see how you got within a mile of her unless you brought the groceries to the back door. But all the rest of that's a God Damned lie. Daisy loved me when she married me and she loves me now."

"No," said Gatsby, shaking his head.

"She does, though. The trouble is that sometimes she gets foolish ideas in her head and doesn't know what she's doing." He nodded sagely. "And what's more, I love Daisy too. Once in a while I go off on a spree and make a fool of myself, but I always come back, and in my heart I love her all the time."

"You're revolting," said Daisy. She turned to me and her voice, dropping an octave lower, filled the room with thrilling scorn: "Do you know why we left Chicago? I'm surprised that they didn't treat you to the story of that little spree."

Gatsby walked over and stood beside her.

"Daisy, that's all over now," he said earnestly. "It doesn't matter any more. Just tell him the truth—that you never loved him—and it's all wiped out forever."

She looked at him blindly. "Why,—how could I love him—possibly?"

"You never loved him."

She hesitated. Her eyes fell on Jordan and me with a sort of appeal, as though she realized at last what she was doing—and as though she had never, all along, intended doing anything at all. But it was done now. It was too late.

"I never loved him," she said, with perceptible reluctance.

"Not at Kapiolani?" demanded Tom suddenly.

"No."

From the ballroom beneath, muffled and suffocating chords were drifting up on hot waves of air.

"Not that day I carried you down from the Punch Bowl to keep your shoes dry?" There was a husky tenderness in his tone. ". . . Daisy?"

"Please don't." Her voice was cold but the rancour was gone from it. She looked at Gatsby. "There, Jay," she said—but her hand as she tried to light a cigarette was trembling. Suddenly she threw the cigarette and the burning match on the carpet.

"Oh, you want too much!" she cried to Gatsby. "I love you now—isn't that enough? I can't help what's past." She began to sob helplessly. "I did love him once—but I loved you too."

Gatsby's eyes opened and closed.

"You loved me *too?*" he repeated.

"Even that's a lie," said Tom savagely. "She didn't know you were alive. Why,—there're things between Daisy and me that you'll never know, things that neither of us can ever forget."

The words seemed to bite physically into Gatsby.

"I want to speak to Daisy alone," he insisted. "She's all excited now——"

"Even alone I can't say I never loved Tom," she admitted in a pitiful voice. "It wouldn't be true."

"Of course it wouldn't," agreed Tom.

She turned to her husband.

"As if it mattered to you," she said.

"Of course it matters. I'm going to take better care of you from now on."

"You don't understand," said Gatsby, with a touch of panic. "You're not going to take care of her any more."

"I'm not?" Tom opened his eyes wide and laughed. He could afford to control himself now. "Why's that?"

"Daisy's leaving you."

"Nonsense."

"I am, though," she said with a visible effort.

"She's not leaving me!" Tom's words suddenly leaned down over Gatsby. "Certainly not for a common swindler who'd have to steal the ring he put on her finger."

"I won't stand this!" cried Daisy. "Oh, please let's get out."

1. What is symbolic about the specific location of this confrontation?

2. At what point does the conflict turn in Tom's favor? Why?

3. How does Daisy's throwing a lighted cigarette to the floor underscore the emotional effect of her words to Gatsby?

4. How do the "muffled and suffocating chords" from the ballroom echo the emotions of the characters in this scene?

5. What do the details of Tom's behavior, including mannerisms and gestures, suggest about his level of confidence in the scene?

Passage 11

She was the first "nice" girl he had ever known. In various unrevealed capacities he had come in contact with such people but always with indiscernible barbed wire between. He found her excitingly desirable. He went to her house, at first with other officers from Camp Taylor, then alone. It amazed him—he had never been in such a beautiful house before. But what gave it an air of breathless intensity was that Daisy lived there—it was as casual a thing to her as his tent out at camp was to him. There was a ripe mystery about it, a hint of bedrooms upstairs more beautiful and cool than other bedrooms, of gay and radiant activities taking place through its corridors and of romances that were not musty and laid away already in lavender but fresh and breathing and redolent of this year's shining motor cars and of dances whose flowers were scarcely withered. It excited him too that many men had already loved Daisy—it increased her value in his eyes. He felt their presence all about the house, pervading the air with the shades and echoes of still vibrant emotions.

But he knew that he was in Daisy's house by a colossal accident. However glorious might be his future as Jay Gatsby, he was at present a penniless young man without a past, and at any moment the invisible cloak of his uniform might slip from his shoulders. So he made the most of his time. He took what he could get, ravenously and unscrupulously—eventually he took Daisy one still October night, took her because he had no real right to touch her hand.

He might have despised himself, for he had certainly taken her under false pretenses. I don't mean that he had traded on his phantom millions, but he had deliberately given Daisy a sense of security; he let her believe that he was a person from much the same strata as herself—that he was fully able to take care of her. As a matter of fact he had no such facilities—he had no comfortable family standing behind him and he was liable at the whim of an impersonal government to be blown anywhere about the world.

But he didn't despise himself and it didn't turn out as he had imagined. He had intended, probably, to take what he could and go—but now he found that he had committed himself to the following of a grail. He knew that Daisy was extraordinary but he didn't realize just how extraordinary a "nice" girl could be. She vanished into her rich house, into her rich, full life, leaving Gatsby—nothing. He felt married to her, that was all.

When they met again two days later it was Gatsby who was breathless, who was somehow betrayed. Her porch was bright with the bought luxury of star-shine; the wicker of the settee squeaked fashionably as she turned toward him and he kissed her curious and lovely mouth. She had caught a cold and it made her voice huskier and more charming than ever and Gatsby was overwhelmingly aware of the youth and mystery that wealth imprisons and preserves, of the freshness of many clothes and of Daisy, gleaming like silver, safe and proud above the hot struggles of the poor.

1. How do the length and syntax of the sentence beginning "There was a ripe mystery about it" emphasize what Gatsby feels about Daisy's house?

2. What literary technique is Fitzgerald using with the words "the invisible cloak" of Gatsby's uniform? In what sense is his uniform such a cloak?

3. What does Fitzgerald imply when he says that "Gatsby took what he could get, ravenously and unscrupulously—eventually he took Daisy one still October night, took her because he had no real right to touch her hand"?

4. What does Fitzgerald mean by the "following of a grail"? What is the literal and figurative meaning of Daisy as a grail?

5. How does adding the words "that was all" affect our understanding of "He felt married to her"?

Passage 12

No telephone message arrived but the butler went without his sleep and waited for it until four o'clock—until long after there was anyone to give it to if it came. I have an idea that Gatsby himself didn't believe it would come and perhaps he no longer cared. If that was true he must have felt that he had lost the old warm world, paid a high price for living too long with a single dream. He must have looked up at an unfamiliar sky through frightening leaves and shivered as he found what a grotesque thing a rose is and how raw the sunlight was upon the scarcely created grass. A new world, material without being real, where poor ghosts, breathing dreams like air, drifted fortuitously about . . . like that ashen, fantastic figure gliding toward him through the amorphous trees.

The chauffeur—he was one of Wolfshiem's protégés—heard the shots—afterward he could only say that he hadn't thought anything much about them. I drove from the station directly to Gatsby's house and my rushing anxiously up the front steps was the first thing that alarmed anyone. But they knew then, I firmly believe. With scarcely a word said, four of us, the chauffeur, butler, gardener and I, hurried down to the pool.

There was a faint, barely perceptible movement of the water as the fresh flow from one end urged its way toward the drain at the other. With little ripples that were hardly the shadows of waves, the laden mattress moved irregularly down the pool. A small gust of wind that scarcely corrugated the surface was enough to disturb its accidental course with its accidental burden. The touch of a cluster of leaves revolved it slowly, tracing, like the leg of a compass, a thin red circle in the water.

It was after we started with Gatsby toward the house that the gardener saw Wilson's body a little way off in the grass, and the holocaust was complete.

1. How does Fitzgerald develop an elegiac tone in this passage?

2. What two points of view are we given in the first paragraph, and where does the shift between them occur? What effect does this shift create?

3. Why is the world Gatsby has lost described as "old" and "warm"?

4. When Daisy doesn't call, why might the sky look "unfamiliar," the leaves "frightening," and a rose "grotesque" to Gatsby?

5. What does it mean for Gatsby's new world to be "material without being real"?

6. Why does Fitzgerald write "started with Gatsby toward the house" rather than "started with Gatsby['s body] toward the house"?

Passage 13

When I left his office the sky had turned dark and I got back to West Egg in a drizzle. After changing my clothes I went next door and found Mr. Gatz walking up and down excitedly in the hall. His pride in his son and in his son's possessions was continually increasing and now he had something to show me.

"Jimmy sent me this picture." He took out his wallet with trembling fingers. "Look there."

It was a photograph of the house, cracked in the corners and dirty with many hands. He pointed out every detail to me eagerly. "Look there!" and then sought admiration from my eyes. He had shown it so often that I think it was more real to him now than the house itself.

"Jimmy sent it to me. I think it's a very pretty picture. It shows up well."

"Very well. Had you seen him lately?"

"He come out to see me two years ago and bought me the house I live in now. Of course we was broke up when he run off from home but I see now there was a reason for it. He knew he had a big future in front of him. And ever since he made a success he was very generous with me."

He seemed reluctant to put away the picture, held it for another minute, lingeringly, before my eyes. Then he returned the wallet and pulled from his pocket a ragged old copy of a book called "Hopalong Cassidy."

"Look here, this is a book he had when he was a boy. It just shows you."

He opened it at the back cover and turned it around for me to see. On the last fly-leaf was printed the word SCHEDULE, and the date September 12th, 1906. And underneath:

Rise from bed	6.00	A.M.
Dumbbell exercise and wall-scaling	6.15–6.30	"
Study electricity, etc.	7.15–8.15	"
Work	8.30–4.30	P.M.
Baseball and sports	4.30–5.00	"
Practice elocution, poise and how to attain it	5.00–6.00	"
Study needed inventions	7.00–9.00	"

GENERAL RESOLVES

No wasting time at Shafters or [a name, indecipherable]

No more smokeing or chewing

Bath every other day

Read one improving book or magazine per week

Save $5.00 [crossed out] $3.00 per week

Be better to parents

"I come across this book by accident," said the old man. "It just shows you, don't it?"

"It just shows you."

"Jimmy was bound to get ahead. He always had some resolves like this or something. Do you notice what he's got about improving his mind? He was always great for that. He told me I et like a hog once and I beat him for it."

He was reluctant to close the book, reading each item aloud and then looking eagerly at me. I think he rather expected me to copy down the list for my own use.

1. For Mr. Gatz, why is the photograph of the house more real than the house itself?

2. What is the significance of *Hopalong Cassidy* as the book containing Gatsby's list of "general resolves"?

3. Does Fitzgerald intend us to view Gatsby's schedule and resolves with admiration or irony?

4. How does Nick's repetition of the phrase "it just shows you" verbatim contribute to the tone of his response to Mr. Gatz?

Passage 14

About five o'clock our procession of three cars reached the cemetery and stopped in a thick drizzle beside the gate—first a motor hearse, horribly black and wet, then Mr. Gatz and the minister and I in the limousine, and, a little later, four or five servants and the postman from West Egg in Gatsby's station wagon, all wet to the skin. As we started through the gate into the cemetery I heard a car stop and then the sound of someone splashing after us over the soggy ground. I looked around. It was the man with owl-eyed glasses whom I had found marvelling over Gatsby's books in the library one night three months before.

I'd never seen him since then. I don't know how he knew about the funeral or even his name. The rain poured down his thick glasses and he took them off and wiped them to see the protecting canvas unrolled from Gatsby's grave.

I tried to think about Gatsby then for a moment but he was already too far away and I could only remember, without resentment, that Daisy hadn't sent a message or a flower. Dimly I heard someone murmur "Blessed are the dead that the rain falls on," and then the owl-eyed man said "Amen to that," in a brave voice.

We straggled down quickly through the rain to the cars. Owl Eyes spoke to me by the gate.

"I couldn't get to the house," he remarked.

"Neither could anybody else."

"Go on!" He started. "Why, my God! they used to go there by the hundreds."

He took off his glasses and wiped them again outside and in.

"The poor son-of-a-bitch," he said.

❧

1. What literary technique is Fitzgerald using when he sets the funeral on a gray, drizzly day? What emotions does the scene arouse?

2. In what way are the "owl-eyed glasses" related to a larger symbolic pattern in the novel?

3. Nick remarks about Owl Eyes, "I don't know how he knew about the funeral or even his name." How does this statement contribute to the symbolic significance of Owl Eyes?

4. How does Nick feel about being "without resentment" at Daisy's not sending a message or flower?

5. What ironies do you observe in the circumstances of Gatsby's funeral?

Passage 15

Most of the big shore places were closed now and there were hardly any lights except the shadowy, moving glow of a ferryboat across the Sound. And as the moon rose higher the inessential houses began to melt away until gradually I became aware of the old island here that flowered once for Dutch sailors' eyes— a fresh, green breast of the new world. Its vanished trees, the trees that had made way for Gatsby's house, had once pandered in whispers to the last and greatest of all human dreams; for a transitory enchanted moment man must have held his breath in the presence of this continent, compelled into an aesthetic contemplation he neither understood nor desired, face to face for the last time in history with something commensurate to his capacity for wonder.

And as I sat there, brooding on the old unknown world, I thought of Gatsby's wonder when he first picked out the green light at the end of Daisy's dock. He had come a long way to this blue lawn and his dream must have seemed so close that he could hardly fail to grasp it. He did not know that it was already behind him, somewhere back in that vast obscurity beyond the city, where the dark fields of the republic rolled on under the night.

Gatsby believed in the green light, the orgastic future that year by year recedes before us. It eluded us then, but that's no matter—tomorrow we will run faster, stretch out our arms farther. . . . And one fine morning——

So we beat on, boats against the current, borne back ceaselessly into the past.

1. In what sense are the houses "inessential"?

2. What group of related symbols culminates with "a fresh, green breast of the new world"?

3. How is it that the trees could have "pandered in whispers to the last and greatest of all human dreams"?

4. How in these last four paragraphs is Gatsby's story transformed into the story of "man . . . face to face for the last time in history with something commensurate to his capacity for wonder"?

5. What does it mean for people to be "boats against the current"?

The Great Gatsby

Suggestions for Writing

❦

Writing about literature is best thought of as an extension of reading and discussion,
as readers return to unresolved questions or investigate unexplored avenues of inquiry.
Readers may also learn and retain more by articulating their ideas
carefully and thoroughly in written form.

Analytical Writing

1. Metaphor and imagery contribute largely to Fitzgerald's distinctive style in *The Great Gatsby*. Write an essay analyzing two or three important metaphors and explaining their contribution to the novel's overall effect.

2. Write an essay analyzing how race is represented in *The Great Gatsby,* paying particular attention to Fitzgerald's portrayal of Jewish and African American characters and to Tom's fascination with early-twentieth-century theories of white superiority.

3. Write an essay analyzing the role of women in *The Great Gatsby,* as represented by Daisy, Jordan, and Myrtle. What kind of influence or power do they wield? Consider their social positions and interactions.

4. Fitzgerald wrote "Winter Dreams" in 1922, three years before *The Great Gatsby* was published. Analyze the ways in which the issues raised in the short story anticipate those of the novel, particularly by comparing and contrasting the characters of Dexter and Gatsby.

5. *The Great Gatsby* has been called "the great American novel." In what sense is the novel about a uniquely American experience? Why does Fitzgerald compare Gatsby's experience to that of the first Dutch sailors who encountered the "new world"?

6. Social class plays a prominent role in *The Great Gatsby*. To what extent does the novel critique class divisions, and to what extent does it endorse them? Specifically, consider Nick's comments about "a sense of the fundamental decencies" being "parceled out unequally at birth" and what Gatsby's rise and fall say about the pursuit of wealth and status in the world of the novel.

7. What hierarchy of values does Fitzgerald establish in *The Great Gatsby*? Based on your reading of the novel, which personal qualities does Fitzgerald prize most highly? Which does he condemn most strongly?

8. To what extent do you think Nick's portrayal of Gatsby in *The Great Gatsby* is objective? To what extent is it shaped by Nick's beliefs, needs, or expectations?

9. Read passage 13 from *The Great Gatsby* and the selection from *The Autobiography of Benjamin Franklin.* Compare and contrast the schedules written by Fitzgerald and Franklin, then write an essay in which you analyze each author's purpose and tone.

Creative/Personal Writing

1. Consider the losses that Nick and Gatsby experience in *The Great Gatsby,* then think of a loss you have experienced. Describe some aspect of it that no one but you could know about.

2. Choose one of the key events that Nick relates in *The Great Gatsby* and briefly retell it from the point of view of one of the other characters, such as Daisy, Jordan, Tom, George, Myrtle, or Gatsby's father.

3. The billboard of Doctor T. J. Eckleburg dominates the valley of ashes in *The Great Gatsby.* Describe an urban or rural landscape that includes a prominent billboard. Use the advertising to suggest an ironic commentary on the scene you depict.

4. *The Great Gatsby* abounds with icons of the 1920s—Gatsby's car, jazz, women's dresses. List some objects that typify the current decade, and then incorporate as many of them as is reasonably possible into a few paragraphs describing a day in your life.

5. In *The Great Gatsby*, Nick is both attracted to and repelled by Gatsby. Have you ever felt that way about someone? What about the person's character caused you to react as you did? Address your contradictory feelings toward that person in a short story or essay.

6. Is trying to do something that may be impossible—such as Gatsby's pursuit of Daisy in *The Great Gatsby*—a valuable or a foolish endeavor? Write an essay or short story in which you or a character pursues a dream that may be unattainable.

7. In *The Great Gatsby*, Nick observes that "Jay Gatsby . . . sprang from his Platonic conception of himself" and that "to this conception he was faithful to the end." Is creating a character for oneself and remaining faithful to it a good or a bad thing? Explore your ideas in a personal essay.

Background and Context

Scholars and historians describe the 1920s in America

as a decade of prosperity, artistic innovation, and

widespread social and political change. These selections

about Prohibition, flappers, jazz, and the leisure class,

along with other aspects of the Roaring Twenties,

offer insights into the era that produced

The Great Gatsby.

Coolidge Prosperity

Frederick Lewis Allen

Business was booming when Warren Harding died, and in a primitive Vermont farmhouse, by the light of an old-fashioned kerosene lamp, Colonel John Coolidge administered to his son Calvin the oath of office as president of the United States. The hopeless depression of 1921 had given way to the hopeful improvement of 1922 and the rushing revival of 1923.

The prices of common stocks, to be sure, suggested no unreasonable optimism. On August 2, 1923, the day of Harding's death, United States Steel (paying a five-dollar dividend) stood at 87, Atchison (paying six dollars) at 95, New York Central (paying seven) at 97, and American Telephone and Telegraph (paying nine) at 122; and the total turnover for the day on the New York Stock Exchange amounted to only a little over 600,000 shares. The big bull market was still far in the future. Nevertheless the tide of prosperity was in full flood.

Pick up one of those graphs with which statisticians measure the economic ups and downs of the postwar decade. You will find that the line of business activity rises to a jagged peak in 1920, drops precipitously into a deep valley in late 1920 and 1921, climbs uncertainly upward through 1922 to another peak at the middle of 1923, dips somewhat in 1924 (but not nearly so far as in 1921), rises again in 1925 and 1926, dips momentarily but slightly toward the end of 1927, and then zigzags up to a perfect Everest of prosperity in 1929—only to plunge down at last into the bottomless abyss of 1930 and 1931.

Hold the graph at arm's length and glance at it again, and you will see that the clefts of 1924 and 1927 are mere indentations in a lofty and irregular plateau that reaches from early 1923 to late 1929. That plateau represents nearly seven years of unparalleled plenty; nearly seven years during which men and women might be disillusioned about politics and religion and love, but believed that at the end of the rainbow there was at least a pot of negotiable legal tender consisting of the profits of American industry and American salesmanship; nearly seven years during which the businessman was, as Stuart Chase put it, "the dictator of our destinies," ousting "the statesman, the priest, the philosopher, as the creator of standards of ethics and behavior" and becoming "the final authority on the conduct of American society." For nearly seven years the prosperity bandwagon rolled down Main Street.

Not everyone could manage to climb aboard this wagon. Mighty few farmers could get so much as a fingerhold upon it. Some dairymen clung there, to be sure, and fruit growers and truck gardeners. For prodigious changes were taking place in the national diet as the result of the public's discovery of the useful vitamin, the propaganda for a more varied menu, and the invention of better methods of shipping perishable foods. Between 1919 and 1926, the national production of milk and milk products increased by one-third and that of ice cream alone took a 45 percent jump. Between 1919 and 1928, as families learned that there were vitamins in celery, spinach, and carrots, and became accustomed to serving fresh vegetables the year round (along with fresh fruits), the acreage of nineteen commercial truck vegetable crops nearly doubled. But the growers of staple crops such as wheat and corn and cotton were in a bad way. Their foreign markets had dwindled under competition from other countries. Women were wearing less and less cotton. Few agricultural raw materials were used in the new economy of automobiles and radios and electricity. And the more efficient the poor farmer became, the more machines he bought to increase his output and thus keep the wolf from the door, the more surely he and his fellows were faced by the specter of over-

New products were portrayed as glamorous.

It hasn't a single belt, fan or drain pipe....

GE Refrigerator
GENERAL ELECTRIC

production. The index number of all farm prices, which had coasted from 205 in 1920 to 116 in 1921—"perhaps the most terrible toboggan slide in all American agricultural history," to quote Stuart Chase again—regained only a fraction of the ground it had lost: in 1927 it stood at 131. Loudly the poor farmers complained, desperately they and their Norrises and Brookharts and Shipsteads and La Follettes campaigned for federal aid, and by the hundreds of thousands they left the farm for the cities.

There were other industries unrepresented in the triumphal march of progress. Coal mining suffered, and textile manufacturing, and shipbuilding, and shoe and leather manufacturing. Whole regions of the country felt the effects of depression in one or more of these industries. The South was held back by cotton, the agricultural Northwest by the dismal condition of the wheat growers, New England by the paralysis of the textile and shoe industries. Nevertheless, the prosperity bandwagon did not lack for occupants, and their good fortune outweighed and outshouted the ill fortune of those who lamented by the roadside.

In a position of honor rode the automobile manufacturer. His hour of destiny had struck. By this time paved roads and repair shops and filling stations had become so plentiful that the motorist might sally forth for the day without fear of being stuck in a mudhole or stranded without benefit of gasoline or crippled by a dead spark plug. Automobiles were now made with such precision, for that matter, that the motorist need hardly know a spark plug by sight; thousands of automobile owners had never even lifted the hood to see what the engine looked like. Now that closed cars were in quantity production, furthermore, the motorist had no need of Spartan blood, even in January. And the stylish new models were a delight to the eye. At the beginning of the decade most cars

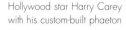

Hollywood star Harry Carey with his custom-built phaeton

had been somber in color, but with the invention of pyroxylin finishes they broke out (in 1925 and 1926) into a whole rainbow of colors, from Florentine cream to Versailles violet. Bodies were swung lower, expert designers sought new harmonies of line, balloon tires came in, and at last even Henry Ford capitulated to style and beauty.

If any sign had been needed of the central place which the automobile had come to occupy in the mind and heart of the average American, it was furnished when the Model A Ford was brought out in December 1927. Since the previous spring, when Henry Ford had shut down his gigantic plant, scrapped his Model T and the thousands of machines that brought it into being, and announced that he was going to put a new car on the market, the country had been in a state of suspense. Obviously he would have to make drastic changes. Model T had been losing to Chevrolet its leadership in the enormous low-priced-car market, for the time had come when people were no longer content with ugliness and a maximum speed of forty or forty-five miles an hour; no longer content, either, to roar slowly uphill with a weary left foot jammed against the low-speed pedal while robin's-egg-blue Chevrolets swept past in second. Yet equally obviously Henry Ford was the mechanical genius of the age. What miracle would he accomplish?

Rumor after rumor broke into the front pages of the newspapers. So intense was the interest that even the fact that an automobile dealer in Brooklyn had "learned something of the new car through a telegram from his brother Henry" was headline stuff. When the editor of the Brighton, Michigan, *Weekly Argus* actually snapped a photograph of a new Ford out for a trial spin, newspaper readers pounced on the picture and avidly discussed its every line. The great day arrived when this newest product of the inventive genius of the age was to be shown to the public. The Ford Motor Company was running in 2,000 daily newspapers a five-day series of full-page advertisements at a total cost of $1,300,000; and everyone who could read was reading them. On December 2, 1927, when Model A was unveiled, one million people—so the *Herald-Tribune* figured—tried to get into the Ford headquarters in New York to catch a glimpse of it; as Charles Merz later reported in his life of Ford, "one hundred thousand people flocked into the showrooms of the Ford Company in Detroit; mounted police were called out to patrol the crowds in Cleveland; in Kansas City so great a mob stormed Convention Hall that platforms had to be built to lift the new car high enough for everyone to see it." So it went from one end of the United States to the other. Thousands of orders piled up on the Ford books for Niagara Blue roadsters and Arabian Sand phaetons.

For weeks and months, every new Ford that appeared on the streets drew a crowd. To the motor-minded American people the first showing of a new kind of automobile was no matter of merely casual or commercial interest. It was one of the great events of the year 1927; not so thrilling as Lindbergh's flight, but rivaling the execution of Sacco and Vanzetti, the Hall-Mills murder trial, the Mississippi

Self-service gas station in the 1920s

flood, and the Dempsey-Tunney fight at Chicago in its capacity to arouse public excitement.

In 1919 there had been 6,771,000 passenger cars in service in the United States; by 1929 there were no less than 23,121,000. There you have possibly the most potent statistic of Coolidge prosperity. As a footnote to it I suggest the following. Even as early as the end of 1923 there were two cars for every three families in "Middletown," a typical American city. The Lynds and their investigators interviewed 123 working-class families of "Middletown" and found that 60 of them had cars. Of these 60, 26 lived in such shabby-looking houses that the investigators thought to ask whether they had bathtubs, and discovered that as many as 21 of the 26 had none. The automobile came even before the tub!

And as it came, it changed the face of America. Villages that had once prospered because they were "on the railroad" languished with economic anemia; villages on Route 61 bloomed with garages, filling stations, hot-dog stands, chicken-dinner restaurants, tearooms, tourists' rests, camping sites, and affluence. The interurban trolley perished, or survived only as a pathetic anachronism. Railroad after railroad gave up its branch lines or saw its revenues slowly dwindling under the competition of mammoth interurban buses and trucks snorting along six-lane concrete highways. The whole country was covered with a network of passenger bus lines. In thousands of towns, at the beginning of the decade a single traffic officer at the junction of Main Street and Central Street had been sufficient for the control of traffic. By the end of the decade, what a difference!—red and green lights, blinkers, one-way streets, boulevard stops, stringent and yet more stringent parking ordinances—and still a shining flow of traffic that backed up for blocks along Main Street every Saturday and Sunday afternoon. Slowly but surely the age of steam was yielding to the gasoline age.

The radio manufacturer occupied a less important seat than the automobile manufacturer on the prosperity bandwagon, but he had the distinction of being the youngest rider. You will remember that there was no such thing as radio-broadcasting to the public until the autumn of 1920, but that by the spring of 1922 radio had become a craze—as much talked about as mahjong was to be the following year or crossword puzzles the year after. In 1922 the sales of radio sets, parts, and accessories amounted to $60,000,000. People wondered what would happen when the edge wore off the novelty of hearing a jazz orchestra in Schenectady or in Davenport, Iowa, play "Mr. Gallagher and Mr. Shean." What actually did happen is suggested by the cold figures of total annual radio sales for the next few years:

1922—$ 60,000,000 (as we have just seen)
1923—$136,000,000
1924—$358,000,000
1925—$430,000,000
1926—$506,000,000
1927—$425,600,000
1928—$650,550,000
1929—$842,548,000 (an increase over the 1922 figures of 1,400 percent!)

Don't hurry past those figures. Study them a moment, remembering that whenever there is a dip in the curve of national prosperity there is likely to be a dip in the sales of almost every popular commodity. There was a dip in national prosperity in 1927, for instance; do you see what it did to radio sales? But there was also a dip in 1924, a worse one in fact. Yet radio sales made in that year the largest proportional increase in the whole period. Why? Well, for one thing, that was the year in which the embattled Democrats met at Madison Square Garden in New York to pick a standard-bearer, and the deadlock between the hosts of McAdoo and the hosts of Al Smith lasted day after day after day, and millions of Americans heard through loudspeakers the lusty cry of, "Alabama, twenty-four votes for Underwoo—ood!" and discovered that a political convention could be a grand show to listen to and that a seat by the radio was as good as a ticket to the Garden. Better, in fact; for at any moment you could turn a knob and get "Barney Google" or "It Ain't Gonna Rain No More" by way of respite. At the age of three-and-a-half years, radiobroadcasting had attained its majority.

Behind those figures of radio sales lies a whole chapter of the life of the post-war decade: radio penetrating every third home in the country; giant broadcasting stations with nationwide hookups; tenement-house roofs covered with forests of antennas; Roxy and his Gang, the Happiness Boys, the A & P Gypsies, and Rudy Vallee crooning from antique Florentine cabinet sets; Graham McNamee's voice, which had become more familiar to the American public than that of any other citizen of the land, shouting across your living room and mine: "And he did it! Yes, sir, he did it! It's a touchdown! Boy, I want to tell you this is one of the finest games . . ."; the government belatedly asserting itself in 1927 to allocate wavelengths among competing radio stations; advertisers paying huge sums for the privilege of introducing Beethoven with a few well-chosen words about yeast or toothpaste; and Michael Meehan personally conducting the common stock of the Radio Corporation of America from a 1928 low of 85 ¼ to a 1929 high of 549.

Charlie Chaplin

There were other riders on the prosperity bandwagon. Rayon, cigarettes, refrigerators, telephones, chemical preparations (especially cosmetics), and electrical devices of various sorts all were in growing demand. While the independent storekeeper struggled to hold his own, the amount of retail business done in chain stores and department stores jumped by leaps and bounds. For every $100 worth of business done in 1919, by 1927 the five-and-ten-cent chains were doing $260 worth, the cigar chains $153 worth, the drug chains $224 worth, and the grocery chains $387 worth. Mrs. Smith no longer patronized her "naborhood" store; she climbed into her two-thousand-dollar car to drive to the red-fronted chain grocery and save twenty-seven cents on her daily purchases. The movies prospered, sending their celluloid reels all over the world and making Charlie Chaplin, Douglas Fairbanks, Gloria Swanson, Rudolph Valentino, and Clara Bow familiar figures to the Eskimo, the Malay, and the heathen Chinese; while at home

Alla Nazimova and
Rudolf Valentino

the attendance at the motion-picture houses of "Middletown" during a single month (December 1923) amounted to four-and-a-half times the entire population of the city. Men, women, and children, rich and poor, the Middletowners went to the movies at an average rate of better than once a week!

Was this Coolidge prosperity real? The farmers did not think so. Perhaps the textile manufacturers did not think so. But the figures of corporation profits and wages and incomes left little room for doubt. Consider, for example, two significant facts at opposite ends of the scale of wealth. Between 1922 and 1927, the purchasing power of American wages increased at the rate of more than two percent annually. And during the three years between 1924 and 1927 alone, there was a leap from 75 to 283 in the number of Americans who paid taxes on income of more than a million dollars a year.

Why did it happen? What made the United States so prosperous?

Some of the reasons were obvious enough. The war had impoverished Europe and hardly damaged the United States at all; when peace came the Americans found themselves the economic masters of the world. Their young country, with enormous resources in materials and in human energy and with a wide domestic market, was ready to take advantage of this situation. It had developed mass production to a new point of mechanical and managerial efficiency. The Ford gospel of high wages, low prices, and standardized manufacture on a basis of the most minute division of machine-tending labor was working smoothly not only at Highland Park, but in thousands of other factories. Executives, remembering with a shudder the piled-up inventories of 1921, had learned the

lesson of cautious hand-to-mouth buying; and they were surrounded with more expert technical consultants, research men, personnel managers, statisticians, and business forecasters than had ever before invaded that cave of the winds, the conference room. Their confidence was strengthened by their almost superstitious belief that the Republican administration was their invincible ally. And they were all of them aided by the boom in the automobile industry. The phenomenal activity of this one part of the body economic—which was responsible, directly or indirectly, for the employment of nearly four million men—pumped new life into all the rest.

More Americans began furnishing their homes on credit.

Prosperity was assisted, too, by two new stimulants to purchasing, each of which mortgaged the future but kept the factories roaring while it was being injected. The first was the increase in installment buying. People were getting to consider it old-fashioned to limit their purchases to the amount of their cash balance; the thing to do was to "exercise their credit." By the latter part of the decade, economists figured that 15 percent of all retail sales were on an installment basis, and that there were some six billions of "easy payment" paper outstanding. The other stimulant was stock market speculation. When stocks were skyrocketing in 1928 and 1929, it is probable that hundreds of thousands of people were buying goods with money that represented, essentially, a gamble on the business profits of the 1930s. It was fun while it lasted.

If these were the principal causes of Coolidge prosperity, the salesman and the advertising man were at least its agents and evangels. Business had learned as never before the immense importance to it of the ultimate consumer. Unless he could be persuaded to buy and buy lavishly, the whole stream of six-cylinder cars, superheterodynes, cigarettes, rouge compacts, and electric iceboxes would be dammed at its outlet. The salesman and the advertising man held the key to this outlet. As competition increased their methods became more strenuous. No longer was it considered enough to recommend one's goods in modest and explicit terms and to place them on the counter in the hope that the ultimate consumer would make up his mind to purchase. The advertiser must plan elaborate national campaigns, consult with psychologists, and employ all the eloquence of poets to cajole, exhort, or intimidate the consumer into buying—to "break down

consumer resistance." Not only was each individual concern struggling to get a larger share of the business in its own field, but whole industries shouted against one another in the public's ear. The embattled candy manufacturers took full-page space in the newspapers to reply to the American Tobacco Company's slogan of "Reach for a Lucky instead of a sweet." Trade journals were quoted by the *Reader's Digest* as reporting the efforts of the furniture manufacturers to make the people "furniture conscious" and of the clothing manufacturers to make them "tuxedo conscious." The salesman must have the ardor of a zealot, must force his way into people's houses by hook or by crook, must let nothing stand between him and the consummation of his sale. As executives put it, "You can't be an order taker any longer—you've got to be a *salesman*." The public, generally speaking, could be relied upon to regard with complacence the most flagrant assaults upon its credulity by the advertiser and the most outrageous invasions of its privacy by the salesman; for the public was in a mood to forgive every sin committed in the holy name of business.

The Age of Play

Robert L. Duffus

The first unmistakable sign of the coming era was the development of interest in games, a phenomenon faintly manifested in the United States for a decade or two prior to the Civil War, and slowly gathering strength thereafter. Baseball first appeared in something like its modern form about 1845, but did not produce its first professionals and thus start on its career as a great national spectacle until 1871. Lawn tennis, first played in America in 1875, and golf, introduced early in the last decade of the century, remained games for the few until very recently [early 1920s]. Now there are said to be 2 million golfers and from a quarter to one-half as many tennis players. These are conspicuous instances of a general tendency. The playing of outdoor games was formerly either a juvenile or an aristocratic diversion; it has now become practically universal. There are golf links upon which horny-handed men in overalls play creditable games. And the number of onlookers at professional sports is legion. In a single year, there are said to have been 17 million admissions to college football games and 27 million to big-league baseball games.

A second phase of the development of play in America is the community recreation movement, which arose from the discovery by social workers that training and organization for leisure were becoming as necessary as training and organization for work. In 1895, the city of Boston took the radical step of providing three sand piles for the entertainment of young children; model playgrounds came about ten years later, and the first "recreation centers" were not established until the middle of the first decade of the budding century. As late as 1903, only eighteen cities had public playgrounds of any description. Then the growth of such facilities began with a rush. Last year there were 6,601 playgrounds in 680 cities, with an average daily attendance of about a million and a half.

In eighty-nine cities there were municipal golf courses on which any man or woman who could afford clubs, balls, and a small green fee could play. Besides golf courses and tennis courts, upon which many a commoner became proficient in what had been "gentlemen's" games, there were municipal swimming pools, ball grounds, theaters, and, in forty-five instances, summer camps under municipal auspices. Municipal expenditures for public recreation have nearly trebled since 1913, though they are as yet only about one-third of the national chewing-gum bill.

But no spontaneous play and no disinterestedly organized recreation program can for a moment be compared in magnitude with what are commonly known as the commercialized amusements—"the greatest industry in America,"

as James Edward Rogers of the Playground and Recreation Association has called them. The motion picture, the phonograph, and the cheap automobile came into existence, like the cheap newspaper, because a public had been created that (consciously or not) wanted them and could pay for them. Each had been the object of experimentation during the last quarter of the nineteenth century, but each attained social significance only after the opening of the twentieth, when multitudes, for the first time in history, had money and leisure they did not know how to use.

The Ballyhoo Years

Frederick Lewis Allen

ll nations, in all eras of history, are swept from time to time by waves of contagious excitement over fads or fashions or dramatic public issues. But the size and frequency of these waves is highly variable, as is the nature of the events that set them in motion. One of the striking characteristics of the era of Coolidge prosperity was the unparalleled rapidity and unanimity with which millions of men and women turned their attention, their talk, and their emotional interest upon a series of tremendous trifles—a heavyweight boxing match, a murder trial, a new automobile model, a transatlantic flight.

Most of the causes célébres that thus stirred the country from end to end were quite unimportant from the traditional point of view of the historian. The future destinies of few people were affected in the slightest by the testimony of the "pig woman" at the Hall-Mills trial or the attempt to rescue Floyd Collins from his Kentucky cave. Yet the fact that such things could engage the hopes and fears of unprecedented numbers of people was anything but unimportant. No account of the Coolidge years would be adequate that did not review that strange procession of events that a nation tired of "important issues" swarmed to watch, or that did not take account of that remarkable chain of circumstances that produced as the hero of the age, not a great public servant, not a reformer, not a warrior, but a stunt flyer who crossed the ocean to win a money prize.

By the time Calvin Coolidge reached the White House, the tension of the earlier years of the postwar decade had been largely relaxed. Though Woodrow Wilson still clung feebly to life in the sunny house in S Street, the League [of

Nations] issue was dead and only handfuls of irreconcilable idealists imagined it to have a chance of resuscitation. The radicals were discouraged, the labor movement had lost energy and prestige since the days of the big Red scare, and under the beneficent influence of easy riches—or at least of easy Fords and Chevrolets—individualistic capitalism had settled itself securely in the saddle. The Ku Klux Klan numbered its millions, yet already it was beginning to lose that naive ardor that had lighted its fires on a thousand hilltops; it was becoming less of a crusade and more of a political racket. Genuine public issues, about which the masses of the population could be induced to feel intensely, were few and far between. There was Prohibition, to be sure—anybody could get excited about Prohibition—but because the division of opinion on liquor cut across party lines, every national politician, almost without exception, did his best to thrust this issue into the background. In the agricultural Northwest and Middle West there was a violent outcry for farm relief, but it could command only a scattered and half-hearted interest throughout the rest of a nation that was

Charles Lindbergh, known as "Lucky Lindy," made the first solo transatlantic flight from New York to Paris in May 1927.

becoming progressively urbanized. Public spirit was at low ebb; over the World Court, the oil scandals, the Nicaraguan situation, the American people as a whole refused to bother themselves. They gave their energies to triumphant business, and for the rest they were in holiday mood. "Happy," they might have said, "is the nation which has no history—and a lot of good shows to watch." They were ready for any good show that came along.

It was now possible in the United States for more people to enjoy the same good show at the same time than in any other land on earth or at any previous time in history. Mass production was not confined to automobiles; there was mass production in news and ideas as well. For the system of easy nationwide communication that had long since made the literate and prosperous American people a nation of faddists was rapidly becoming more widely extended, more centralized, and more effective than ever before.

To begin with, there were fewer newspapers, with larger circulation, and they were standardized to an unprecedented degree by the increasing use of press association material and syndicated features. Between 1914 and 1926, as Silas

Publisher William
Randolph Hearst

Bent has pointed out, the number of daily papers in the country dropped from 2,580 to 2,001, the number of Sunday papers dropped from 571 to 541, and the aggregate circulation per issue rose from somewhat over 28,000,000 to 36,000,000. The city of Cleveland, which a quarter of a century before had had three morning papers, now had but one; Detroit, Minneapolis, and St. Louis had lost all but one apiece; Chicago, during a period in which it had doubled in population, had seen the number of its morning dailies drop from seven to two. Newspapers all over the country were being gathered into chains under more or less centralized direction: by 1927 the success of the Hearst and Scripps Howard systems and the hope of cutting down overhead costs had led to the formation of no less than 55 chains controlling 230 daily papers with a combined circulation of over 13,000,000.

No longer did the local editor rely as before upon local writers and cartoonists to fill out his pages and give them a local flavor; the central office of the chain, or newspaper syndicates in New York, could provide him with editorials, health talks, comic strips, sob-sister columns, household hints, sports gossip, and Sunday features prepared for a national audience and guaranteed to tickle the mass mind. Andy Gump and Dorothy Dix had their millions of admirers from Maine to Oregon, and the words hammered out by a reporter at Jack Dempsey's training camp were devoured with one accord by real-estate men in Florida and riveters in Seattle.

Meanwhile, the number of national magazines with huge circulations had increased, the volume of national advertising had increased, a horde of publicity agents had learned the knack of associating their cause or product with whatever happened to be in the public mind at the moment, and finally there was the new and vastly important phenomenon of radiobroadcasting, which on occasion could link together a multitude of firesides to hear the story of a World Series game or a Lindbergh welcome. The national mind had become as never before an instrument upon which a few men could play. And these men were learning, as Mr. Bent has also shown, to play upon it in a new way—to concentrate upon *one tune at a time*.

Not that they put their heads together and deliberately decided to do this. Circumstances and self-interest made it the almost inevitable thing for them to do. They discovered—the successful tabloids were daily teaching them—that the public tended to become excited about one thing at a time. Newspaper owners and editors found that whenever a Dayton trial or a *Vestris* disaster took place, they sold more papers if they gave it all they had—their star reporters, their front-page display, and the bulk of their space. They took full advantage of this discovery: according to Mr. Bent's compilations, the insignificant Gray-Snyder murder trial got a bigger "play" in the press than the sinking of the *Titanic;* Lindbergh's flight, than the armistice and the overthrow of the German Empire. Syndicate managers and writers, advertisers, press agents, radiobroadcasters, all were aware that mention of the leading event of the day, whatever it might be, was the key to public interest. The result was that when something happened that promised to appeal to the popular mind, one had it hurled at one in huge headlines, waded through page after page of syndicated discussion of it, heard about it on the radio, was reminded of it again and again in the outpourings of publicity-seeking orators and preachers, saw pictures of it in the Sunday papers and in the

movies, and (unless one was a perverse individualist) enjoyed the sensation of vibrating to the same chord that thrilled a vast populace.

The country had bread, but it wanted circuses—and now it could go to them a hundred million strong.

The *New York Daily News* sensationalized the 1928 execution of Ruth Snyder with this front-page photograph, the first of a woman's electrocution.

The Flourishing of Jazz

Michael Brooks

J azz began as a music associated with dancing, and it remained that way as it moved into the 1920s, with one overriding difference: In earlier years, live jazz, still in embryonic form, was hard to find outside of New Orleans and a few other cities. But in the 1920s, it took shape as a distinct musical style known and embraced by young audiences the world over.

Its first creative geniuses—Louis Armstrong, Duke Ellington, Sidney Bechet, and Jelly Roll Morton—produced key work during the twenties, transforming what had once been a rough iteration of ragtime, the blues, and marching music into an art of sophistication and depth. Through vision and force of personality, they established new artistic benchmarks and conventions that would last through the remainder of the century: Where jazz had once been an ensemble sound, artists in the wake of Armstrong shifted the focus to soloists. Where jazz composition had formerly been narrowly conceived, new artists envisioned it as broader, more open-ended. Where band sounds had been limited, innovators expanded the sonic palette, introducing new timbres and combinations of instruments. And making their accomplishment all the more remarkable was the fact that they did it in the restrictive sphere of popular entertainment, where the first order of business was to keep the crowds coming.

Nightlife and the surrounding social whirl, whatever the creative limitations it placed on performers,

Louis Armstrong with his band, the Hot Five, in 1925

had everything to do with jazz coming into public favor. New trends in the use of leisure time—trends that favored the public consumption of music—had emerged in the years surrounding and during World War I. Burgeoning and diversifying populations in urban industrial centers, combined with changing social attitudes, had spiked demand for new kinds and places of entertainment. A dance craze swept U.S. cities from 1912 to 1916, fueled by a new permissiveness that made public dancing socially acceptable for both women and men. The opening of New York City's Roseland Ballroom in 1919 heralded a boom in dancehalls in the 1920s, and dance bands played for young people who wanted to forget the war and instead look forward to a brighter future.

Duke Ellington

With the passage of the Volstead Act in 1919, Prohibition had come into force, outlawing the manufacture and sale of alcohol. But instead of eliminating consumption, Prohibition drove it underground, where nightclubs, cabarets, and speakeasies lured late-night crowds with the promise of illegal booze and unregulated revelry.

The Roaring Twenties, with its taste for the new, the exciting, and the exotic, found in jazz the perfect sonic accompaniment. So great a part of the cultural fabric was the new music that novelist F. Scott Fitzgerald dubbed the 1920s the Jazz Age.

Jazz also rode in on the coattails of a growing white fascination with African American culture. In August 1920, singer Mamie Smith made the first blues record, *Crazy Blues,* which opened the floodgates for "race records"—discs made expressly for blacks, but that whites also purchased. In New York, the home of the largest concentration of African Americans in the United States, all-black revues and musicals were the rage on Broadway, fueling a market for other types of black entertainment and art. But even more key was the explosion of interest in African American–derived dancing. One 1923 revue, *Runnin' Wild,* popularized the Charleston. The step became a national fad for several years and created a vogue for other dances—and for the jazz that accompanied them.

Further laying the groundwork for the spread and development of jazz in the 1920s were advances in communications and recording technology. Radio became a mass medium in the middle part of the decade, exposing listeners all over the United States to the sound of the new music. At the same time, phonograph recording shifted from acoustic to electrical reproduction techniques, vastly improving the quality of recorded sound and inspiring such jazz composers as Duke Ellington to create more detailed and intricate musical arrangements.

In the 1920s, New York remained the center of the entertainment industry, but, thanks to a still-vital vaudeville circuit, musical acts spread across the country on lengthy tours, bringing up-to-date entertainment into any town large enough to have a theater. Jazz, too, especially as black musicians moved north and east from the economically waning South, found its way into other cities. Chief among them were Chicago and Kansas City.

One of the great attractions of Harlem's nightlife in the 1920s was the Cotton Club, an illegal drinking establishment and forum for aspiring jazz artists.

The Evolution of
the Flapper

Elizabeth Stevenson

The opportunities and the pressures of a new age created new kinds of people. Whether or not there was freedom and a new chance for all—and there was not—there existed an erroneous but cheering belief that there was change ahead. The openness of the future and the accessibility, as it seemed, of success produced a froth upon the times, and many short-lived, heedless, sometimes graceful, careers danced upon this foam of confidence. A later, more solid time that would have more real opportunity would lack this effervescence, which was a unique attribute of the twenties. An English observer characterized a conspicuous part of the population: "Dancing as aimlessly as gnats in winter sunshine it brings to bear on the jolly business of being *ephemeridae* the same hard and cheerful efficiency that it uses in its moneymaking." Observers from overseas were keen, but never got it quite right. They assumed in Americans a hard, deliberate choice in the universal career of moneymaking with other choices discarded, whereas, for Americans, there was nothing else they knew, and they put into moneymaking the traits reserved in Europe for other careers: sports, gambling, politics, status creation, even remotely, a kind of aesthetics.

The most effervescent symbol of the twenties was the flapper. She was a new American girl, a new woman, a new arrangement of the elements of sex and love. She no longer exists; she existed for only a few years in the mid and late twenties, but during that short epoch she was a completely defined and recognizable type. In the twenties she was suddenly there, it seemed, and welcome.

Yet the flapper evolved. She was born perhaps in the experiences some few women had in the war of 1917–18, when all sorts of freedoms and equalities with men occurred during the exigencies of Red Cross and other welfare work among the soldiers or particularly in the excitements of entertaining them. Travel, informality, closeness of contact between the two sexes in situations of danger changed the relations between men and women, at least for short periods in certain places; and some of this carried over into the period after the war, buried at first, but asserting itself at last with impudence and self-assurance.

Mary Pickford was not a flapper, and the Mary Pickford type of sweet, confiding, shy, and yet gay innocent female dominated the early after-the-war covers and illustrations in *The Saturday Evening Post,* which may be taken as a place to

watch for the flapper's arrival. A change appears first in the familiarity of the boy and girl on the innocuous covers. In a Norman Rockwell painting for the issue of March 12, 1921, the girl is more kittenish than hoydenish; her hair, her dress, her attitude are soft and tentative, but she is unafraid and a little bold, whereas the boy whose hand she is holding—to tell his fortune—is awkward. She looks into his eyes with confidence and no assumption of consequences to her boldness. A year later, in a cover by Thomas H. Webb for the issue of May 13, 1922, the closeness of the boy and the girl, while still playful, is more self-conscious; he is standing close in an attitude of embrace, ostensibly showing her how to hold a bow and arrow; her dress is beginning to be tomboyish: a skirt and sweater, the sweater belted in leather, an Indian beaded band across her forehead. Her glance backward at the young man—awkward boy no longer—is more conscious of possible consequences of this exciting intimacy.

During 1922 and 1923, the girls in the stories still wear soft, full dresses, rather awkwardly long. Sometimes the heroine in sweater and skirt wears her hair in a long, thick braid down her back. Older women wear ample clothes, which denote maturity. In 1924, there is a change in an occasional cover or illustration. Out of the cover of January 5, 1924, a gambling girl looks straight at you. Her dress is the slightest, flimsiest silk, cut low and square-necked, thin straps over her shoulders. Her bobbed hair is almost hidden by a soft, wide, shirred bandeau of the same silken material as the slight, slim gown. She handles gambling counters as she sits at a table; the look she gives says that she handles her life as a gamble, too.

. . . As late as January 1925, a cover shows a fond and fatuous portrait of a Mary Pickford girl who has long corkscrew curls trailing down to a soft and modest neckline. But inside the same issue, on the first page after the cover, there is a bold girl in a hosiery ad who seems to herald a new age. She is perched carelessly but gracefully upon a glossy mahogany table, dangling one silken leg off the edge. Her hair is softly waved and bobbed and her dress is sleeveless and short, held up by straps that look like flowers. Her slippers are slight things with pointed toes. At this moment the flapper is here, and all girls, the good ones and the bad ones, try to be flappers; the time is the end of the year 1925 and the early part of 1926. So long did it take her to come. Girls with skirts short to the knees or just below the knees become frequent if not universal.

In a story in the issue of April 3, 1926, there is a girl who is the very type: a girl seen in a careless pose, her back to us, on tiptoes, her dress hem hitting the back of her knees, her waist low and bloused. On her head is a cloche hat with a soft brim. Another story shows the same kind of girl dancing the Charleston, the caption comments, "with imagination and abandon." Girls, by this time, are shown putting on lipstick in public, confident of their own importance, and displaying a breezy independence of opinion. Many girls try to be flappers. The generic flapper is the nice girl who is a little fast, who takes the breath of staid observers with her flip spontaneity, her short-lived likes and dislikes, her way of skating gaily over thin ice. Would-be flappers are often heartless little ignoramuses, gum-chewing, vulgar, wearing ridiculous clothes, imitating a mode in second-rate style; others are overdecorated, costly, gangsters' girlfriends. Many girls of the midtwenties, however, grew up, finished school, fell in love, married, all without any whiff of the style of the type—yet bobbing their hair, doing up their hems, learning to Charleston.

By 1925, the phenomenon of the flapper was so conspicuous that many words were put on paper analyzing her. In 1920, before the full-blown type existed, Scott Fitzgerald gave a book of short stories the title *Flappers and Philosophers.* A magazine like *The New Republic,* given to the serious study of politics and economics, had space on September 9, 1925, for a piece by Bruce Bliven, an attempt to describe the new girl. Bliven thought he knew how she made up her face and what she wore and told it in a piece called "Flapper Jane":

> She is frankly, heavily made-up, not to imitate nature, but for an altogether artificial effect—pallor mortis, poisonously scarlet lips, richly

ringed eyes—the latter looking not so much debauched (which is the intention) as diabetic. . . .

[Her clothes] . . . were estimated the other day by some statistician to weigh two pounds. Probably a libel; I doubt if they come within half a pound of such bulk. Jane isn't wearing much this summer. If you'd like to know exactly, it is: one dress, one step-in, two stockings, two shoes. [No petticoat, no brassiere, of course, no corset.]

The flapper seemed the most notable new character upon the scene. She attracted the most attention. When she smoked a cigarette conspicuously on a public street, reporters made a front-page story of the incident. She rallied a whole new circle of male types around her. Her beaus, boys in Joe College clothes, or sharp young gentlemen in belted jackets and new Van Heusen soft collars, and trousers with wide flapping legs, shared her good times, learning to drink in a dry age, dancing the fox trot in roadhouses, riding about in rattletrap flivvers or expensive Marmons, going to the movies and the speakeasies, traveling across the Atlantic to a gay, superficial Europe that seemed to belong to

John Held Jr.'s illustrations for *Life* magazine captured the spirit of the age.

Americans. Oddly, the particular, identifiable flapper faded away very quickly, to be replaced, so that the fact was hardly noticed, by another. She and her boyfriend, after a short season of gaiety, a year or two or more, vanished and became part of a solid, respectable, and inconspicuous mass of settled, older, married folks, upholding the standards of the good life as sketched so preposterously and winningly in Sinclair Lewis's *Babbitt*. Flappers and Babbitts had to be rather well off. Unprosperous folks did not have the time or cash to belong to either type, so the double layer of gay young people and stuffily proper middle-aged ones was after all very thin, the two-tiered icing upon the cake of the age.

Playing Along the Danger Line: Women in the 1920s

Sheila Rowbotham

High society in Montgomery, Alabama, turned out as usual for the annual masked ball, Les Mystérieuses, in 1921. That year an especially daring dancer held the floor dressed in a brief grass skirt. With every eye upon her, she lifted her skirt over her head and gave a final provocative wiggle: "A murmur went over the auditorium in a wave of excitement and everybody was whispering 'That's Zelda!' . . ."

Zelda Fitzgerald, a new-style rebel southern belle, was presented by her novelist husband, Scott Fitzgerald, as the personification of the 1920s flapper, "flirting, kissing, viewing life lightly, saying damn without a blush, playing along the danger line in an immature way—a sort of mental baby vamp." Though she appeared to be playing the part with zest, the two partners were to remember this period in their lives very differently. He said in the early 1930s, "We were about the most envied couple . . . in America," to which she replied, "I guess so. We were awfully good showmen."

After more than a decade of emotional battling, his drinking, and her mental illness, Scott Fitzgerald told his wife, "I would like you to think of my interests. That is your primary concern, because I am the one to steer the course, the pilot," and when she asked him what he wanted her to do, he responded emphatically, "I want you to stop writing fiction." Zelda Fitzgerald, who had wanted to be "mistress of her own fate" by being lighthearted and unconventional, had rejected the dreary option of the "emancipation" of an older generation because she thought that all it brought was "a career that calls for hard work, intellectual pessimism, and loneliness." She was to discover in her turn that love, freedom, and fulfillment were elusive bedfellows.

The 1920s flapper frantically dancing and experimenting with sex was partly a chimera created by the media. The new independent woman appears lighting up Lucky Strike cigarettes or triumphantly riding the waves in a Coca-Cola advertisement of 1923. Ads like these were actually a response to the personal rebellion and consumer power that had emerged in the preceding decade, when flapper habits had upset moralists. The media of the 1920s was, however, able to

The new woman was self-reliant.

transmit flapper styles on a mass scale. But it was not simply a matter of image and style, for behind all the razzmatazz a genuine sense of confusion existed about how to be a modern woman. In 1922 Freda Kirchwey defined herself as a "left-wing feminist and internationalist." But this could not resolve inward uncertainties. In *Our Changing Morality* in 1924, she observed how the modern woman found "the old rules fail to work; bewildering inconsistencies confront her. . . . Slowly, clumsily she is trying to construct a way out to a new sort of certainty in life."

This restless quest for identity was most intense among white, upper-middle-class, educated young women, many of whom turned to psychoanalysis for enlightenment. However, sexual rebellion and the aspiration for personal autonomy had a wider influence. *Las pelonas* (the bobbed-haired girls) feature in a verse from a corrido in the Los Angeles Mexican community in the 1920s. The "flappers" stroll out for a good time in their straw hats after the harvesting and cotton picking is done. Families divided over bobbed hair and bathing suits. An older Mexicano remembers telling his daughter, "You can bathe at home. I will educate you . . . but [I will] not buy a bathing suit. You can wait till I am dead and buy it then."

The sexual dynamics of rebellion had, however, different social meanings. Young black women intellectuals, for instance, encountered a complex series of restraints upon a purely sexual personal search for autonomy. Respectability and education were vital in their struggle for freedom. Hazel Carby points out that novelists like Jessie Fauset "faced a very real contradiction . . . if they acknowledged their sexuality and sensuality," for this simply got them branded in racist terms as "primitive and exotic creatures."

Bessie and Sadie Delany were always conscious that they were being watched and judged by whites as representatives of the young black intelligentsia. When they moved to Harlem, they were surrounded by the ferment of the Harlem Renaissance. However, Sadie commented in *Having Our Say,* "Being good girls, Bessie and I did not venture too far into the jazz scene. After all, we were Bishop Delany's daughters." Bessie, however, did throw herself into the debates about race, politics, and culture. Rejecting the moderate Booker T. Washington, "a smoother of the waters," for the more militant strategy of W. E. B. Du Bois, she marched in so many protests "it's a wonder I didn't wear out my feet." Like other educated black women, she recollects, "I was torn between two issues—colored and women's rights. But it seemed to me that no matter how much I had to put up with as a woman, the bigger problem was being colored." Nonetheless, the day women got the right to vote in 1920 was one of the happiest days of her life.

Maude Russell (center) and the "Ten Ebony Steppers" in a Broadway show

The Bootlegger

Joseph K. Willing

With the advent of the Volstead Act, a new occupation or "profession" opened for thousands of Americans: that of bootlegging, *a term that apparently originated in the southern hills from the practice of illegal still operators carrying their goods to consumers in the top of their boots. But bootlegging in the twenties was a much more complex industry, running from a one-man manufacturing operation to those headed by an organization worthy of a large legitimate corporation. An assistant district attorney of Philadelphia, Joseph K. Willing, discusses the new profession in its many aspects.*

he specific subject that I have been asked to discuss is the "profession of bootlegging." When my mind first attacked this subtitle, it asked itself, what is a profession? I resorted immediately to the dictionaries and found it to be generally described as a phase of human endeavor, openly avowed by one who has become expert by reason of special scholastic training. The latest Funk & Wagnalls dictionary is the only one that seems to know anything about bootlegging. Whatever is said about it there implies that there is a sort of antinomy between the word *profession* as defined above and bootlegging as it is generally practiced and known. Bootlegging has none of the characteristics of the definition, except that it seems to be a new line of human endeavor. It is, however, not openly avowed and requires no scholastic education nor academic sanction.

It is presumed that the word *bootlegging* comes from a practice in some of the southern states where the moonshiner sought to avoid the payment of the federal tax on manufactured distilled spirits. The moonshiner would deliver his pint or half-pint in the leg of his boot and this article of wearing apparel may be described as the first vehicle used in the transportation of intoxicating liquor, even antedating the hip pocket. Whatever be the historical antinomy inherent in the title chosen, it seems that the public at large is prepared to recognize a new profession, and to require no academic degrees for its candidates. This new profession wrings from the bosom of Mammon many more shekels than its legitimate brethren. Let us now turn to a consideration of its characteristics.

Like all professions in this modern age, it has become specialized, and the specialties arrange themselves in the following categories:

    I.   Smuggling and transportation
   II.   Redistillation or recooking
  III.   Doctor and druggist complex
  IV.   Brewing of high-power beer
   V.   Home brew and accessory stores
  VI.   Homemade wine, ciders, and cordials

Opposite: An illegal still used to manufacture bootleg liquor

To state the divisions of the profession is to say almost all that need be said about them. They have become so well known that the public can be said to take judicial notice of their content.

Authorities empty barrels of confiscated beer into the street.

Profile of a Bootlegger

Edward Behr

With Prohibition, America was all set for a wild drinking spree that would last thirteen years, five months, and nine days. It would transform the country's morals, alter American attitudes toward law enforcers, politicians, and all those in authority, and herald a new mood of cynicism, along with an often justified conviction that the courts dispensed a form of two-tier justice based on class, wealth, and rank. And even if the Prohibition phenomenon itself, which was largely responsible for this general, unfocused resentment, was soon forgotten, for other reasons the mood of distrust has persisted to this day.

The Prohibition era has been chronicled in hundreds of films and classics, such as F. Scott Fitzgerald's *The Great Gatsby*. Underworld figures such as Al Capone, catapulted onto the world scene by Prohibition, became in time mythic heroes, as did the bootleggers' nemesis, Eliot Ness.

Eliot Ness

But the political immorality in high places that allowed the lawbreakers to flourish—and that marked the 1920s in other ways—has been largely ignored or forgotten. It is as if those Americans who experienced the Prohibition years were determined to put them out of their minds as soon as it was repealed. Their reaction was understandable. Compared to the years of the Harding presidency, at the beginning of Prohibition (1920–1923), major scandals such as those that brought about the collapse of the Italian Christian Democratic hegemony looked like trifling peccadilloes.

For gangsters, bootleggers, and speakeasies to flourish, the liquor had to come from somewhere. The story of George Remus, the German-born American who became the richest bootlegger of all, shows how simple it was to lay one's hands on almost limitless quantities of whiskey without resorting to rumrunners or homemade stills—and often without even formally breaking the law.

Remus exemplified the new breed of American. His father, Franck Remus (who dropped the Germanic spelling of his first name after immigrating to America), came from Friedberg, near Berlin. The history of the Remus family is a textbook illustration of the appalling health hazards prevalent in the nineteenth century. Franck's parents both died a few weeks after his birth, probably from cholera, and he subsequently became an apprentice in a woolen mill. There, he did well, marrying Maria Karg, the mill owner's daughter, in 1871. They had three girls, but all died in infancy. Their fourth child, George Remus, lived, and when he was four and a half years old, the three of them left for Milwaukee, then almost a German enclave, where several members of the Karg family had already settled.

In Milwaukee, tragedy continued to dog the Remus family. Maria gave birth to two more sons, who also died in infancy. She then had three more children, all girls, who lived, followed by a third son, Herman, who, as a child, was hit on the back of the head by a flying brick and as a result became mentally unstable. He died in 1918.

A couple is scrutinized at the entrance to a speakeasy.

Try as they might, the panel of psychiatrists who, at the request of the court, examined George Remus before his trial and spent hours debriefing him on his antecedents, found "no record of suicidal or criminal tendencies upon the part of any member of this family." "None of the family could be called 'alcoholic,'" the panel wrote, "although many of them, as is common with their countrymen, drank considerable beer. George Remus's father drank only moderately, usually on Saturdays."

George was a good child in every way, an older sister, Mrs. Gabriel Ryerson, told the panel, "talkative, energetic, a book lover, careful in his appearance, and very seldom had to be scolded. He always looked on the bright side of things and had a sense of humor." Although Remus himself remained a lifelong teetotaler and nonsmoker, he was "fond of parties, always celebrating good news or success, dismissing discomforts of all kinds with feelings of lightheartedness. Irritations were never of long duration." Although he was quick-tempered, his sister recalled, he was affectionate, made friends easily, and had a natural sense of responsibility, even as a child. He had been confirmed in the Lutheran Church (though neither George Remus nor his family was particularly religious), but was sufficiently intrigued by the dogma of various churches to attend Catholic,

Presbyterian, and occasionally Christian Science church services. Apparently, none fully satisfied him. "My religion," he told the panel, "is to pay my obligations and keep my word." He was "dubious about the hereafter and did not worry much about it." Despite his short, stocky build (in his early photographs he resembles Danny De Vito; in his later ones, Mussolini) and his one indulgence— good food—he became a strong swimmer and a much-sought-after member of the Illinois Athletic Club's water polo team. The examining psychiatrists found him "alert, friendly, courteous and perfectly willing to cooperate in every way."

As Remus told the panel, despite his mother's relatively prosperous background, his family fell on hard times shortly after settling in Milwaukee. Frank, no longer a weaver but a lumber scorer, became crippled with articular rheumatism, a virtual invalid no longer able to work.

They left for Chicago, and soon young George Remus, still in his early teens, became the family's mainstay. An uncle, George Karg, had a drugstore there, and George left school to work as his assistant. When his uncle decided to sell his shop, George obtained a bank loan and bought and ran the store himself, with a much increased profit. He was only nineteen, but had by this time become a licensed pharmacologist (by making himself out to be older than he was). He never graduated, displaying, as a student, the same headstrong qualities that were to plague him in later life. Just before his final examination, he led a student walkout to protest the behavior of an unpopular teacher, and when the teacher took his revenge, handing out punitive low grades, Remus never returned to school.

A Prohibition-era poster depicting temperance crusader Carry Nation

This in no way, however, prevented him from prospering. From the profits of his first shop, he bought a second drugstore near Milwaukee Avenue. He also became a certified optometrist, and his examining panel noted that he "indulged in the practice of medicine in connection with his drugstore among the people of his neighborhood." The practice was common among pharmacists; doctors were expensive, and there was no social security. Among his clients was a neighbor, Lillian Kraus. They fell in love, married, and had a daughter, Romola. In the somewhat dated jargon of the times, the panel noted that "his sexual life showed no perversities."

George Remus, in his twenties, found time not only to run two drugstores, write out prescriptions for glasses, act as an unlicensed doctor, and raise a family, but to study law at night school. At age twenty-four, he was admitted to the Illinois Bar and started his own practice. From the very start, he was successful. He specialized in criminal law, but also actively represented several Chicago labor unions and made quite a name for himself as a divorce lawyer. A well-known local figure with many Democratic connections, Remus was several times approached and asked to stand for local political office. "I could easily have become a district attorney," he told the panel. "I was prominent enough politically to secure public office, but have never wanted to take the prosecutor's side in my life." In light of his many achievements, it is somewhat surprising that at the time of his murder trial, when they submitted him to various tests, including those standard 1920s examinations the Stanford Revision of the Binet-Simon Scale and the Otis Self-Administering Test of Mental Ability, the psychiatrists examining him found George Remus to be "of only average adult intelligence." They did add that "the possibility that this record may have been lowered by mental distraction at the time of the examination should not be overlooked."

Remus hired a legal secretary, Imogene Holmes, a young divorcée with a small daughter, Ruth. Imogene, a remarkably strong, graceful swimmer, was a voluptuous woman with somewhat extravagant tastes in clothes and unusual hats. Little is known of her family background, though she boasted to George Remus that she came "from the top drawer." Remus divorced Lillian in 1917, but continued to support her, remaining on good terms with her and their daughter, Romola, who adored him.

Al Capone

Chicago became dry in 1918. In this hugely corrupt city, where underworld characters immediately became bootleggers, Remus, the criminal lawyer they knew and trusted, was much in demand. Among his clients was Johnny Torrio, a nightclub and brothel owner and one of the first Chicago bootleggers and speakeasy kings. Torrio, himself a strait-laced family man and practicing Catholic despite his many brothel ownerships, summoned one of his distant New York relatives, Alfonso Caponi,[1] to assist him in his operations. Remus knew Capone, too, but only slightly. His acquaintanceship with the Chicago under-world was strictly professional: many of its minor members had visited his office at 167 North Clark Street, on the Chicago Loop, some of them on murder charges. It was because as defense counsel he had been compelled to witness the capital executions of some of his clients (in the electric chair) that he came out strongly against the death penalty. Clarence Darrow, the best-known criminal lawyer in America, also a Chicago colleague, spoke highly of his abilities.

As a brilliant lawyer and an ex-pharmacist, Remus was uniquely qualified to make a fortune out of the Volstead Act. In a series of articles about him in the

---

[1] [*Alfonso Caponi:* This spelling of Al Capone's name is a common misconception; his given name was Alphonse Capone.]

St. Louis Post-Dispatch ("The Inside Story of the Amazing Career of George Remus, millionaire bootlegger and his band of rumrunners," *St. Louis Post-Dispatch*, January 3–20, 1926), Paul Y. Anderson wrote:

> If there has ever been a bigger bootlegger than Remus, the fact remains a secret. . . . Remus was to bootlegging what Rockefeller was to oil. In the sheer imagination of his plan, in the insolent sweep of his ambition and power with which he swept upward toward his goal, Remus can bear comparison with the captains of industry.

Remus told Anderson how the idea came to him. If gangsters of limited intelligence could make a fortune, "Remus could surely do better than they."

His first step was to sell his law practice (though he remained a member of the Bar Association). He then moved, with Imogene, to Cincinnati, where they got married. It was a shrewd move: most of America's whiskey distilleries were within three hundred miles of the town, and Remus knew that despite the wartime ban on grain supplies, the distilleries operating in America and producing an annual output of 286 million gallons had virtually limitless bonded stocks at their disposal. He also knew it was a seller's market: in 1917, the last "normal" year before Prohibition became law in several major states, Americans had consumed two billion gallons of hard liquor. Although some distillers sent their liquor stocks abroad before 1920, hundreds of millions of gallons remained in distilleries and government-bonded warehouses, most of them within easy reach of Cincinnati. In addition, because of Prohibition, "whiskey certificates" were worth next to nothing.

Entirely legally, using his life savings ($100,000), Remus started buying up certificates. His operations became lucrative quickly, and he was soon able to acquire entire distilleries, complete with offices, machinery, furniture, and even abandoned corner saloons, for which he did not have the slightest use. In time, Remus became the largest owner of distilleries in America, his properties including famous brand names: Fleischmann, Old Lexington Club, Rugby, Greendale, and Squibb, the largest in the country. The Fleischmann Distillery, which cost him $197,000, came with 3,100 barrels of prime rye whiskey.

The next step was to get official permission to remove the whiskey and—again quite legally—sell it to drug companies licensed to sell medicinal whiskey. "I started out buying a retail drugstore in Cincinnati and converting it into a wholesale drug company," Remus told the *Post-Dispatch*. "As soon as that company had withdrawn as much liquor as possible without attracting undue attention, I organized another wholesale company, closed up the first one, and shipped the stock of drugs off to the second one. We made that carload of drugs serve as the stock for three or four wholesale companies." Surplus nonalcoholic stocks were "fired off into space" (Anderson's words) to fictitious buyers, eventually sold off as unclaimed freight. In the first few months of Prohibition, Remus set up over a dozen drug companies, closing them down when they began attracting the curiosity of enforcement agents and inventing new ones. When the regulations changed, as they soon did, to limit liquor acquisitions on the part of drug companies to 10 percent of their business, Remus simply cooked the books, showing a huge imaginary turnover.

Once in the hands of the drug companies, some of the whiskey duly ended up in pint bottles labeled "medicinal whiskey," but most of it ended up elsewhere, in the hands of bootleggers, nightclub owners, middlemen, and in exceptional cases, a carefully vetted private clientele. Only a small proportion ended up as "straight" medicinal whiskey—the bootleggers and private customers a far more lucrative market. Anderson wrote that "once out from under the eye of the government, the disposal of whiskey at fabulous prices became a simple matter. The whiskey market is always a seller's market. The supply never equals the demand. Remus's associates already had made contacts with retail bootleggers who would snap up all the good liquor that could be furnished, and would pay eighty dollars a case and upward. There are twelve quarts, or three gallons, to a case. Remus paid from sixty-five cents to four dollars (per case) for the certificates."

"What was wrong with that?" George Conners, Remus's closest associate, asked Anderson. "If anything was wrong it was wrong for the government to destroy the value of those people's property without compensating them for it. If the government wanted to abolish whiskey drinking, why didn't it buy all this whiskey and dump it in the river?" Conners told Anderson he had not intended to get into the whiskey business, "but after several of these fellows came to me, I asked Remus what he would charge me for liquor in fifteen- or twenty-case lots." Remus suggested he think big and quoted a price for 250-case lots. This was the start of the Remus-Conners bootleg operation on a grand scale, with Conners handling sales on a commission basis and drumming up business all over America.

"We never poisoned anybody. We sold good liquor and didn't cut it," Remus told Anderson. This and his meticulously run operation—involving shippers, drivers, bodyguards, and accountants (at his peak there were three thousand people on his payroll)—went far to explain Remus's meteoric career. Within a few months of Prohibition, he was depositing tens of thousands of dollars a day into various bank accounts both in his own name and under aliases.

Remus had one innocuous weakness: he wanted to become a respected member of Cincinnati society. He set about it with his usual thoroughness. First he bought a huge property on Price Hill, overlooking the town, at Eighth and Hermosa Avenue, in what was then its most desirable suburb. Then, regardless of expense (it cost him $750,000, or close to several million dollars today), he had the place remodeled, furnished in somewhat garish taste, and on its extensive grounds built a greenhouse, a racing stable (he soon owned a string of racing thoroughbreds), a landscaped garden, and a series of outhouses. All but one were for his many servants, chauffeurs, and their families, but the largest housed a specially built, Olympic-size indoor swimming pool. This alone cost him another $100,000 (1920).

Much later, when Remus's mansion was demolished, two tunnels were discovered. Remus had had these built to store whiskey for his parties and as a pos-

George Remus's indoor swimming pool, made of Italian marble

sible getaway. "We found many empty bottles there," said Jack Doll, who, as a child and neighbor, had played in Remus's garden, had used the pool, and later was present when the mansion was pulled down. Doll would remember Remus with affection: he was friendly, welcomed poor children on his premises, and, though the property was surrounded by a chainlink fence to keep the racehorses

Imogene Remus, 1922

from straying, instructed his gardener to leave a space so that the local kids could squeeze under it to come and play. Doll remembers Remus playfully pushing a ten-year-old into the pool fully clothed and then giving him a ten-dollar bill "to buy a new suit." "You could buy a whole boy's outfit for a dollar in those days," Doll noted.

As soon as the house was ready, Remus started giving lavish parties. While Cincinnati old money either stayed away or made snide remarks behind his back while enjoying his hospitality, almost all found his invitations irresistible. At formal dinners (the dining room table was big enough to seat twenty in comfort), Remus slipped $100 bills under his guests' plates. On March 21, 1921, at a party staged to celebrate the completion of his swimming pool, he presented all of his guests with gold-engraved Elgin watches as well as photographs of the occasion, taken by a specially hired photographer.

Two years later, in July of 1923, Remus, though by this time in serious trouble with the Justice Department, staged what was even by his standards an extraordinarily elaborate dancing and swimming party. The hundred guests were entertained by a fifteen-piece orchestra and a water ballet, with Imogene Remus, herself a talented swimmer, making a guest appearance in a daringly cut swimsuit. Remus had bought up the stock of a bankrupt Cincinnati jeweler for twenty-five thousand dollars, and upon arrival, all of the female guests got rings, and the males diamond tie clasps. On leaving, in the early hours of the morning, there was another surprise waiting: each female guest (there were fifty in all) was presented with a brand-new 1923 Pontiac. The descendant of one of the assiduous partygoers recalled his parents saying that on these occasions Remus himself was a discreet, almost invisible host. Exploring the mansion during the 1923 extravaganza, they came across him in his library, alone, reading a book and reluctant to be disturbed.

This quest for social respectability at almost any cost was shared by many leading bootleggers elsewhere. Lucky Luciano (in his posthumous memoirs) recalled with obvious pride how he had mingled with Wall Street tycoons such as banker Julie Bach, attended lavish parties given on the estate of the famous Whitney family, and ingratiated himself with over a hundred top socialites, police officials, and politicians by providing them, at huge cost, with black-market tickets to the 1923 Jack Dempsey–Luis Angel Firpo fight at the New York Polo Grounds.

Remus did not confine his parties to his home. There were elaborate lunch parties in his downtown Cincinnati office (on the corner of Race and Pearl Streets), with a butler and chef in constant attendance. Also in 1923, he gave a memorable birthday party for Imogene (also attended by hundreds of guests) in the ballroom of one of Cincinnati's most famous hotels, the Sinton.

Some of Remus's social activities were chronicled in the Cincinnati papers (though the 1923 swimming pool party was not), and he became a household name so quickly that F. Scott Fitzgerald may well have been inspired by him. In many respects, the real-life Remus and the fictional Gatsby were similar. Both were self-made men, both gave lavish parties, both despised their guests' venality, and both were low-key hosts, observing rather than dominating the party scene. There was, however, a major difference between them. Remus, in 1923, was happily married—an adoring husband and doting father who lavished every type of expensive gift on Imogene's daughter, Ruth, including a gold-plated grand piano—whereas Gatsby was a loner, at heart an unrequited romantic.

Remus behind bars. He served five sentences for violating liquor laws.

Conspicuous Consumption

Thorstein Veblen

During the earlier stages of economic development, consumption of goods without stint, especially consumption of the better grades of goods—ideally all consumption in excess of the subsistence minimum—pertains normally to the leisure class. This restriction tends to disappear, at least formally, after the later peaceable stage has been reached, with private ownership of goods and an industrial system based on wage labor or on the petty household economy. But during the earlier quasi-peaceable stage, when so many of the traditions through which the institution of a leisure class has affected the economic life of later times were taking form and consistency, this principle has had the force of a conventional law. It has served as the norm to which consumption has tended to conform, and any appreciable departure from it is to be regarded as an aberrant form, sure to be eliminated sooner or later in the further course of development.

The quasi-peaceable gentleman of leisure, then, not only consumes of the staff of life beyond the minimum required for subsistence and physical efficiency, but his consumption also undergoes a specialization as regards the quality of the goods consumed. He consumes freely and of the best, in food, drink, narcotics, shelter, services, ornaments, apparel, weapons and accouterments, amusements, amulets, and idols or divinities. In the process of gradual amelioration that takes place in the articles of his consumption, the motive principle and the proximate aim of innovation is no doubt the higher efficiency of the improved and more elaborate products for personal comfort and well-being. But that does not remain the sole purpose of their consumption. The canon of reputability is at hand and seizes upon such innovations as are, according to its standard, fit to survive. Since the consumption of these more excellent goods is an evidence of wealth, it becomes honorific; and conversely, the failure to consume in due quantity and quality becomes a mark of inferiority and demerit.

This growth of punctilious discrimination as to qualitative excellence in eating, drinking, etc., presently affects not only the manner of life, but also the training and intellectual activity of the gentleman of leisure. He is no longer simply the successful, aggressive male—the man of strength, resource, and intrepidity. In order to avoid stultification he must also cultivate his tastes, for it now becomes incumbent on him to discriminate with some nicety between the noble and the ignoble in consumable goods. He becomes a connoisseur in creditable viands of various degrees of merit, in manly beverages and trinkets, in seemly apparel and architecture, in weapons, games, dancers, and the narcotics. This cultivation of the aesthetic faculty requires time and application, and the demands made upon

the gentleman in this direction therefore tend to change his life of leisure into a more or less arduous application to the business of learning how to live a life of ostensible leisure in a becoming way. Closely related to the requirement that the gentleman must consume freely and of the right kind of goods, there is the requirement that he must know how to consume them in a seemly manner. His life of leisure must be conducted in due form. Hence arise good manners. . . . Highbred manners and ways of living are items of conformity to the norm of conspicuous leisure and conspicuous consumption.

Conspicuous consumption of valuable goods is a means of reputability to the gentleman of leisure. As wealth accumulates on his hands, his own unaided effort will not avail to sufficiently put his opulence in evidence by this method. The aid of friends and competitors is therefore brought in by resorting to the giving of valuable presents and expensive feasts and entertainments. Presents and feasts had probably another origin than that of naive ostentation, but they acquired their utility for this purpose very early, and they have retained that character to the present, so that their utility in this respect has now long been the substantial ground on which these usages rest. Costly entertainments, such as the potlatch or the ball, are peculiarly adapted to serve this end. The competitor with whom the entertainer wishes to institute a comparison is, by this method, made to serve as a means to the end. He consumes vicariously for his host at the same time that he is a witness to the consumption of that excess of good things that his host is unable to dispose of single-handed, and he is also made to witness his host's facility in etiquette.

In the giving of costly entertainments, other motives, of a more genial kind, are of course also present. The custom of festive gatherings probably originated in motives of conviviality and religion; these motives are also present in the later development, but they do not continue to be the sole motives. The latter-day leisure-class festivities and entertainments may continue in some slight degree to serve the religious need and in a higher degree the needs of recreation and conviviality, but they also serve an invidious purpose, and they serve it none the less

Times Square, circa 1925

effectually for having a colorable noninvidious ground in these more avowable motives. But the economic effect of these social amenities is not therefore lessened, either in the vicarious consumption of goods or in the exhibition of difficult and costly achievements in etiquette.

As wealth accumulates, the leisure class develops further in function and structure, and there arises a differentiation within the class. There is a more or less elaborate system of rank and grades. This differentiation is furthered by the inheritance of wealth and the consequent inheritance of gentility. With the inheritance of gentility goes the inheritance of obligatory leisure, and gentility of a sufficient potency to entail a life of leisure may be inherited without the complement of wealth required to maintain a dignified leisure. Gentle blood may be transmitted without goods enough to afford a reputably free consumption at one's ease. Hence results a class of impecunious gentlemen of leisure, incidentally referred to already. These half-caste gentlemen of leisure fall into a system of hierarchical gradations. Those who stand near the higher and the highest grades of the wealthy leisure class, in point of birth, or in point of wealth, or both, outrank the remoter-born and the pecuniarily weaker. These lower grades, especially the impecunious, or marginal, gentlemen of leisure, affiliate themselves by a system of dependence or fealty to the great ones; by so doing they gain an increment of repute, or of the means with which to lead a life of leisure, from their patron. They become his courtiers or retainers, servants, and being fed and countenanced by their patron, they are indices of his rank and vicarious consumers of his superfluous wealth. Many of these affiliated gentlemen of leisure are at the same time lesser men of substance in their own right, so that some of them are scarcely at all, others only partially, to be rated as vicarious consumers. So many of them, however, as make up the retainers and hangers-on of the patron may be classed as vicarious consumers without qualification. Many of these again, and also many of the other aristocracy of less degree, have in turn attached to their persons a more or less comprehensive group of vicarious consumers in the persons of their wives and children, their servants, retainers, etc.

Alienation and Social Classes

Karl Marx

he proletariat and wealth are opposites. As such they form a whole. They are both products of the world of private property. The whole question is what position each of these two elements occupies within the opposition. It does not suffice to proclaim them two sides of one whole.

Private property as private property, as wealth, is compelled to preserve *its own existence* and thereby the existence of its opposite, the proletariat. This is the *positive* side of the antagonism, private property satisfied with itself.

The proletariat, on the other hand, is compelled to abolish itself and thereby its conditioning opposite—private property—which makes it a proletariat. This is the *negative* side of the antagonism, its disturbance within itself, private property abolished and in the process of abolishing itself.

The possessing class and the proletarian class represent one and the same human self-alienation. But the former feels satisfied and affirmed in this self-alienation, experiences the alienation as a sign *of its own power,* and possesses in it the *appearance* of a human existence. The latter, however, feels destroyed in this alienation, seeing in it its own impotence and the reality of an inhuman existence. To use Hegel's expression, this class is, within depravity, an *indignation* against this depravity, an indignation necessarily aroused in this class by the contradiction between its human *nature* and its life situation, which is a blatant, outright, and all-embracing denial of that very nature.

Within the antagonism as a whole, therefore, private property represents the *conservative* side and the proletariat the *destructive* side. From the former comes

135

action aimed at preserving the antagonism; from the latter, action aimed at its destruction.

In its economic movement, it is true, private property presses toward its own dissolution, but it does this only by means of a developmental course that is unconscious and takes place independently of it and against its will, a course determined by the nature of the thing itself. It does this only by giving rise to the proletariat *as* proletariat—this poverty conscious of its own spiritual and physical poverty, this dehumanization that is conscious of itself as a dehumanization and hence abolishes itself. The proletariat executes the sentence that proletariat-producing private property passes upon itself, just as it executes the sentence that wage labor passes upon itself by producing others' wealth and its own poverty. When the proletariat wins victory, it by no means becomes the absolute side of society, for it wins victory only by abolishing itself and its opposite. Both the proletariat itself and its conditioning opposite—private property—disappear with the victory of the proletariat.

Charlie Chaplin suffers alienation from the means of production in *Modern Times*.

The Horatio Alger Myth

Ralph D. Gardner

he Alger Hero . . . has become a part of our language. As a synonym for spectacular rise to fame and wealth, it has an immediate sight identification that few, if any, other names imply. For who upon hearing the phrase "a typical Alger Hero" does not immediately anticipate a report on the uniquely American phenomenon of one who started from scratch and—generally against great odds—reached the top rung of the ladder?

Isn't it strange, then, that so little is known today about Horatio Alger and his works?

In lectures to American studies groups at various universities, I often start with a question: "Who was Horatio Alger?"

"A poor boy who worked hard and grew up to become a millionaire."

"The name of the hero of a long series of stories."

"A pen name of Charles Dickens."

Author Horatio Alger

Although some know the answer, replies frequently fall short of the target. Rest assured that Horatio Alger was the real name of a real person. Born at Chelsea, Massachusetts, on Friday, January 13, 1832, he authored more than one hundred stories that were printed in scores of editions and multimillions of copies during the half-century between our civil war and World War I. Even after his death in 1899, Alger titles were being read and reread, bought, borrowed, and swapped. Libraries displayed double rows of these fast-moving adventure tales. They were favorite gifts, awarded as school prizes and recommended in sermons. It is safe to assume that there was a very long period during which most boys—

and many girls—who were brought up in the United States enjoyed Alger. He was, without doubt, America's all-time best-selling author!

But there are critics who protest that Horatio Alger was an overrated fraud. He misled kids, they claim, probably causing many who stood up to the neighborhood bully to wind up with a bloody nose. Paul Gallico once wrote that Alger so frightened children with threats of the sinister village squire foreclosing the mortgage that they grew up fearful of mortgages although they didn't really know why they were afraid or what they were afraid of.

We hear from some whose comments are even more crushing. They cling to the fiction that after a heartbreaking college romance that was shattered by his father, Alger rebounded to become a mid-Victorian playboy who chased a Parisian cabaret singer and an English hussy through the hills of Montmartre. In later years, their fantasy persists, he was a pathetically inept adulterer. This may be the stuff from which more recent antihero tales are made, but it is contradicted by facts.

Ragged Dick was an overnight sensation.

Records indicate, rather, that Horatio Alger Jr.—he always signed his name that way—was the oldest of five children of a debt-ridden New England parson. A sickly infant affected all his life by bronchial asthma, he couldn't talk until his seventh year. Nevertheless, he became an honor student at Harvard, a magazine and newspaper editor in Boston, and a teacher. After graduating from the Divinity School at Cambridge, in 1860, he traveled to Europe as a correspondent for the *New York Sun* and the *Boston Transcript*. Returning shortly after the attack upon Fort Sumter, Alger tried to enlist in the Union Army but, due to his bronchial condition (and perhaps, too, because he stood only slightly over five feet tall), was three times rejected. Halfheartedly, he then accepted the pulpit of the First Parish Unitarian Church at Brewster, Massachusetts, resigning less than two years later and moving to New York to pursue a full-time career as a writer.

Since his Harvard days, when he was both a student and disciple of Henry Wadsworth Longfellow, he submitted dozens of bittersweet poems to then popular periodicals. Finding the poetry market limited, he turned to short stories, encouraged by William T. Adams, who, as Oliver Optic, was an author and the editor of *Student and Schoolmate,* the monthly in which *Ragged Dick* was serialized in 1867.

Ragged Dick; or, Street Life in New York was not Alger's first book (it was his eighth), but it was the one that set the pattern for dozens of hero fiction plots he produced at the rate of three or four annually over the next three decades. It was an overnight sensation and, when issued as a book the following year by the Boston publisher A. K. Loring, established Horatio Alger as a major writer for young people.

Dick, a Huckleberry Finn of the Bowery, was a homeless bootblack. He gambled, swigged shots of whiskey at two cents a glass, relished an evening at Barnum's Museum or the Old Bowery Theater, and treated himself to a cigar when he had the extra penny to spare. Alger sometimes supplied such flaws to avoid crowning his lads with a halo or risking them being judged too good to be true. Needless to say, Dick reformed before many chapters pass. Then, defeating schemes of a variety of evildoers, aided by kindly benefactors and with generous dollops of luck and pluck, he spun through a dozen adventures. By story's end, pleased with his self-improvement, a growing bank account, and a good job, Dick told his chum, Fosdick, that he was keeping his box and brushes "to remind me of the hard times I've had when I was an ignorant bootblack and never expected anything better."

"When, in short, you were 'Ragged Dick.' You must drop that name, and think of yourself now as—"

"Richard Hunter, esquire," said our hero, smiling.

"A young gentleman on the way to fame and fortune," added Fosdick.

Dick's friends were then invited to follow his progress in *Fame and Fortune,* the second volume of the series.

Although Alger—who made no pretense to literary genius—wove these stories from similar fabric, he altered patterns sufficiently to keep his readers happily anticipating the next arrival. Actually, he employed four basic themes.

There was, like Ragged Dick, the city waif—an orphan of uncertain background. There was the recently orphaned country boy forced to leave home to seek his fortune in the city. Alger varied some narratives with the addition of a careworn, widowed mother and sometimes a dependent brother or sister. Several heroes were kidnapped in infancy from wealthy homes and loving parents to be reared as tramps, slum urchins, or poorhouse scullions. Of course, they ultimately learned their true identities. In any number of these stories, a culprit was trying to swindle the hero of an inheritance, usually mining or railroad stocks.

Alger liked to describe his young men as being about sixteen years old, not handsome but physically attractive. Hector Roscoe, in *Hector's Inheritance,* was "slenderly but strongly made, with a clear skin and dark eyes and a straightforward look. He had a winning smile that attracted all who saw it, but his face could assume a different expression, if need be. There were strong lines around his mouth that indicated calm resolution and strength of purpose. He was not a boy who would allow himself to be imposed upon, but was properly tenacious of his rights." Scott Walton, in *The Young Salesman,* was "the picture of health. He was inclined to be dark, with black hair, bright eyes, and with considerable color in his cheeks." Ben Stanton, *The Young Explorer,* was "strong and self-reliant . . . his limbs active, and his face ruddy with health. He looked like a boy who could get along. He was not a sensitive plant, and not to be discouraged by rebuffs."

The bootblack Dick eventually becomes a wealthy man.

Alger designed his hero as the boy he wished he himself could have been. They often were dark complexioned, described as "swarthy." Besides fictional characters, he portrayed Daniel Webster and Abraham Lincoln as swarthy in his biographies of them.

Alger customarily thrust the hero upon Lower Broadway with but a few cents in his pocket. Though ragged, he was bright, ambitious, and aggressive and cheerfully accepted a menial station as bootblack, newsboy, or peddler. From the beginning, he had enemies—the swaggering snob, the criminally inclined guardian, the street-corner bully, the traveling con man, the pickpocket, burglar, and kidnapper.

Scoundrels conspired to waylay the hero by chloroform, slugging, drugging, or shanghaiing. They tried to steal his wallet, and he was occasionally thrown into an abandoned well. Between daring escapes, he performed heroic deeds, rescuing a child from the path of a runaway horse, jumping into the East River to save a life, flagging down a speeding train, or preventing an old man from being blackjacked and robbed.

He was rewarded with cash (which was wisely invested) and a better job, perhaps as a clerk earning as much as ten dollars a week. Because he showed initiative and shrewdness, he was sent on a confidential and perilous journey. This mission was always a triumph, and in its course he may have discovered some secret that cleared up the mystery of his own identity or accidentally met the man who helped recover his legacy. While the hero most often had not achieved great wealth, he was well on his way with the clouds past and a bright future predicted at the inevitable happy ending.

Alger was partial to alliterative titles, some of his most popular being *Sink or Swim, Try and Trust, Rough and Ready, Brave and Bold, Slow and Sure,* and *Strive and Succeed.* Heroes were named Frank Fowler, Mark Mason, Bob Burton, and Tom Tracy. There were more than a hundred of them, and they all strived and succeeded.

Horatio Alger's literary quality, modern critics complain, was meager, to say the least. The Alger Hero often was cloyingly virtuous, his rise from rags to riches too often based upon incredible luck. And all he ever cared about was making money! Without attempting to equate Alger's unique product with that of a Herman Melville, a Nathaniel Hawthorne, or a Stephen Crane, it is reasonable to suggest that millions who were enchanted by his stories in times gone by would disagree. Too often his works are examined in the light of late-twentieth-century standards, and in Alger's case, such judgment may be inappropriate. During the 1860s and 1870s, our ancestors readily accepted slower-moving vehicles than the jet aircraft we now use. We wouldn't plan a trip in those fragile covered wagons or buggies, but in their own time they were considered dependable, practical ways to travel. Evaluating Horatio Alger's unsophisticated museum pieces by current rules is about the same as judging horse-drawn shays by criteria set for jet aircraft.

In any event, there seems to be no lack of diverging opinions. Russel Crouse called these works "literary murder," while a *New York Times* editorial named Alger "the Prose Laureate" of juvenile writers. Westbrook Pegler denounced Alger's heroes as "sanctimonious little heels," but Heywood Broun admired these "simple tales of honesty triumphant." S. N. Behrman, rediscovering an Alger story he had cherished years before, simply declared: "I don't know any comparable reading experience; it is like taking a shower in sheer innocence." . . .

His incredible naiveté notwithstanding, few will disagree that Horatio Alger was a novelist of tremendous influence. For youngsters on farms and in teeming cities he provided repeatedly acknowledged incentives to struggle upward. His stories' magic effect upon many was their own resolve that "if Ragged Dick could do it, so can I!" . . .

Try to ascertain how many of Alger's books were printed during his long reign, and you'll come up with astonishing numbers. Although his popularity began to wane during World War I, his books remained in print, profusely, through the 1920s. Street & Smith continued their long-running Alger series, listing some forty titles, well into the 1930s. Estimated totals range from a high of 400,000,000—a figure that is questioned—downward to the 250,000,000 claimed by Quentin Reynolds in his history of Street & Smith, the 200,000,000 quoted in a *New York Times Magazine* article, or the relatively modest 100,000,000 copies suggested by Frederick Lewis Allen. Because most of Alger's more than five dozen publishers went out of business years ago, the exact quantity will never be known. But even the most conservative of these estimates would still be phenomenal!

All Alger's heroes were self-made men.

The Autobiography of
Benjamin Franklin

(selection)

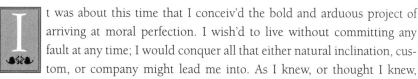t was about this time that I conceiv'd the bold and arduous project of arriving at moral perfection. I wish'd to live without committing any fault at any time; I would conquer all that either natural inclination, custom, or company might lead me into. As I knew, or thought I knew, what was right and wrong, I did not see why I might not *always* do the one and avoid the other. But I soon found I had undertaken a task of more difficulty than I had imagined. While my *attention was taken up* in guarding against one fault, I was often surpris'd by another. Habit took the advantage of inattention. Inclination was sometimes too strong for reason. I concluded at length that the mere speculative conviction that it was our interest to be completely virtuous was not sufficient to prevent our slipping, and that the contrary habits must be broken and good ones acquired and established before we can have any dependence on a steady, uniform rectitude of conduct. For this purpose I therefore contriv'd the following method.

In the various enumerations of the moral virtues I had met with in my reading, I found the catalogue more or less numerous, as different writers included more or fewer ideas under the same name. *Temperance,* for example, was by some confin'd to eating & drinking, while by others it was extended to mean the moderating of every other pleasure, appetite, inclination, or passion, bodily or mental, even to our avarice & ambition. I propos'd to myself, for the sake of clearness, to use rather more names with fewer ideas annex'd to each, than a few names with more ideas; and I included under thirteen names of virtues all that at that time occurr'd to me as necessary or desirable, and annex'd to each a short precept, which fully express'd the extent I gave to its meaning.

These names of virtues with their precepts were:

1. Temperance.
   Eat not to dullness. Drink not to elevation.

2. Silence.
   Speak not but what may benefit others or yourself.
   Avoid trifling conversation.

3. Order.
   Let all your things have their places. Let each part of your
   business have its time.

4. Resolution.
   Resolve to perform what you ought. Perform without fail
   what you resolve.

5. Frugality.
   Make no expense but to do good to others or yourself:
   i.e., waste nothing.

6. Industry.
   Lose no time. Be always employ'd in something useful.
   Cut off all unnecessary actions.

7. Sincerity.
   Use no hurtful deceit. Think innocently and justly; and,
   if you speak, speak accordingly.

8. Justice.
   Wrong none, by doing injuries or omitting the benefits
   that are your duty.

9. Moderation.
   Avoid extremes. Forbear resenting injuries so much as you
   think they deserve.

10. Cleanliness.
    Tolerate no uncleanness in body, clothes, or habitation.

11. Tranquillity.
Be not disturbed at trifles, or at accidents common or unavoidable.

12. Chastity.
Rarely use venery but for health or offspring—never to dullness, weakness, or the injury of your own or another's peace or reputation.

13. Humility.
Imitate Jesus and Socrates.

My intention being to acquire the *habitude* of all these virtues, I judg'd it would be well not to distract my attention by attempting the whole at once, but to fix it on one of them at a time, and when I should be master of that, then to proceed to another, and so on till I should have gone through the thirteen. And as the previous acquisition of some might facilitate the acquisition of certain others, I arrang'd them with that view as they stand above. *Temperance* first, as it tends to procure that coolness & clearness of head, which is so necessary where constant vigilance was to be kept up, and guard maintained, against the unremitting attraction of ancient habits, and the force of perpetual temptations. This being acquir'd & establish'd, *Silence* would be more easy, and my desire being to gain knowledge at the same time that I improv'd in virtue, and considering that in conversation it was obtain'd rather by the use of the ears than of the tongue, & therefore wishing to break a habit I was getting into of prattling, punning, & joking, which only made me acceptable to trifling company, I gave *Silence* the second place. This, and the next, *Order,* I expected would allow me more time for attending to my project and my studies. *Resolution,* once become habitual, would keep me firm in my endeavors to obtain all the subsequent virtues. *Frugality & Industry,* by freeing me from my remaining debt, & producing affluence & independence, would make more easy the practice of *Sincerity* and *Justice,* etc., etc. Conceiving then that, agreeable to the advice of Pythagoras in his Golden Verses, daily examination would be necessary, I contriv'd the following method for conducting that examination.

I made a little book in which I allotted a page for each of the virtues. I rul'd each page with red ink, so as to have seven columns, one for each day of the week, marking each column with a letter for the day. I cross'd these columns with thirteen red lines, marking the beginning of each line with the first letter of one of the virtues, on which line & in its proper column I might mark by a little black spot every fault I found upon examination to have been committed respecting that virtue upon that day.

I determined to give a week's strict attention to each of the virtues successively. Thus in the first week my great guard was to avoid every the least offense against *Temperance,* leaving the other virtues to their ordinary chance, only marking every evening the faults of the day. Thus if in the first week I could keep my first line marked *T* clear of spots, I suppos'd the habit of that virtue so much strengthen'd and its opposite weaken'd, that I might venture extending my attention to include the next, and for the following week keep both lines clear of spots. Proceeding thus to the last, I could go through a course complete in thirteen weeks, and four courses in a year. And like him who, having a garden to weed, does not attempt to eradicate all the bad herbs at once, which would exceed his reach and his strength, but works on one of the beds at a time, & having accomplish'd the first proceeds to a second; so I should have, (I hoped) the encouraging pleasure of seeing on my pages the progress I made in virtue, by clearing successively my lines of their spots, till in the end by a number of courses, I should be happy in viewing a clean book after a thirteen weeks' daily examination.

This, my little book, had for its motto these lines from Addison's *Cato:*

> Here will I hold: If there is a Pow'r above us,
> (And that there is, all Nature cries aloud
> Thro' all her works) he must delight in virtue,
> And that which he delights in must be happy.

FORM OF THE PAGES

Temperance.							
Eat not to dullness. *Drink not to elevation.*							
	S	M	T	W	T	F	S
T							
S	••	•		•		•	
O	•	•	•		•	•	•
R			•			•	
F		•			•		
I		•					
S							
J							
M							
Cl.							
T							
Ch.							
H							

Another from Cicero:

O vitae Philosophia dux! O virtutum indagatrix, expultrixque vitiorum! Unus dies bene, & ex preceptis tuis actus, peccanti immortalitati est anteponendus.

Another from the Proverbs of Solomon speaking of wisdom or virtue:

Length of days is in her right hand, and in her left hand riches and honors; Her ways are ways of pleasantness, and all her paths are peace.

Proverbs 3:16, 17

And conceiving God to be the fountain of wisdom, I thought it right and necessary to solicit his assistance for obtaining it; to this end I form'd the following little prayer, which was prefix'd to my tables of examination, for daily use:

O Powerful Goodness! Bountiful Father! Merciful Guide! Increase in me that wisdom which discovers my truest interests; strengthen my resolutions to perform what that wisdom dictates. Accept my kind offices to thy other children, as the only return in my power for thy continual favors to me.

I us'd also sometimes a little prayer which I took from Thomson's poems, viz.:

> Father of light and life, thou Good supreme,
> O teach me what is good, teach me thy self!
> Save me from folly, vanity, and vice,
> From every low pursuit, and fill my soul
> With knowledge, conscious peace, & virtue pure,
> Sacred, substantial, neverfading bliss!

The precept of *Order* requiring that *every part of my business should have its allotted time,* one page in my little book contain'd the following scheme of employment for the twenty-four hours of a natural day:

Morning question: What good shall I do this day?	5 6 7	Rise, wash, and address Powerful Goodness; contrive day's business and take the resolution of the day; prosecute the present study; and breakfast?
	8 9 10 11	Work.
	12 1	Read, or overlook my accounts, and dine.
	2 3 4 5	Work.
	6 7 8 9	Put things in their places; supper, music, or diversion, or conversation. Examination of the day.
Evening question: What good have I done today?	10 11 12 1 2 3 4	Sleep.

I enter'd upon the execution of this plan for self-examination, and continu'd it with occasional intermissions for some time. I was surpris'd to find myself so much fuller of faults than I had imagined, but I had the satisfaction of seeing them diminish. To avoid the trouble of renewing now & then my little book, which by scraping out the marks on the paper of old faults to make room for new ones in a new course became full of holes, I transferr'd my tables & precepts to the ivory leaves of a memorandum book on which the lines were drawn with red ink that made a durable stain, and on those lines I mark'd my faults with a black lead pencil, which marks I could easily wipe out with a wet sponge. After a while I went through one course only in a year, and afterward only one in several years, till at length I omitted them entirely, being employ'd in voyages & business abroad with a multiplicity of affairs, that interfered, but I always carried my little book with me.

F. Scott Fitzgerald wrote the following letters to Maxwell Perkins, his editor at Scribners, about the publication of *The Great Gatsby*. They are transcribed exactly as Fitzgerald wrote them; no editorial corrections have been made.
If the original letter was not dated, the date has been added in brackets.

Selected Letters

F. Scott Fitzgerald

October 27th, 1924
Villa Marie, Valescure St. Raphael, France
(After Nov. 3d Care of American Express Co, Rome Italy)

Dear Max:

Under separate cover I'm sending you my third novel:

The Great Gatsby

(I think that at last I've done something really my own), but how good "my own" is remains to be seen.

I should suggest the following contract.

15% up to 50,000

20% after 50,000

The book is only a little over fifty thousand words long but I believe, as you know, that Whitney Darrow has the wrong psychology about prices (and about what class constitute the bookbuying public now that the lowbrows go to the movies) and I'm anxious to charge two dollars for it and have it a full size book.

Of course I want the binding to be absolutely uniform with my other books—the stamping too—and the jacket we discussed before. This time I don't want any signed blurbs on the jacket—not Mencken's or Lewis' or Howard's or anyone's. I'm tired of being the author of This Side of Paradise and I want to start over.

About serialization. I am bound under contract to show it to Hearsts but I am asking a prohibitive price, Long hates me and its not a very serialized book. If they should take it—they won't—it would put of publication in the fall. Otherwise you can publish it in the spring. When Hearst turns it down I'm going to offer it to Liberty for $15,000 on condition that they'll publish it in ten weekly installments before April 15th. If they don't want it I shan't serialize. <u>I am absolutely positive Long won't want it</u>.

I have an alternative title:

<u>Gold-hatted Gatsby</u>

After you've read the book let me know what you think about the title. Naturally I won't get a nights sleep until I hear from you but do tell me the absolute truth, <u>your first impression of the book</u> + tell me anything that bothers you in it.

As Ever
Scott

I'd rather you wouldn't call Reynolds as he might try to act as my agent. Would you send me the N.Y. World with accounts of Harvard-Princeton and Yale-Princeton games?

[c. November 7, 1924]
Hotel Continental, St. Raphael, Sun.
(Leaving Tuesday)

Dear Max:

By now you've recieved the novel. There are things in it I'm not satisfied with in the middle of the book—Chapters 6 + 7. And I may write in a complete new scene in proof. I hope you got my telegram.

<u>Trimalchio in West Egg</u>

The only other titles that seem to fit it are <u>Trimalchio</u> and <u>On the Road to West Egg</u>. I had two others <u>Gold-hatted Gatsby</u> and <u>The High-bouncing Lover</u> but they seemed too light.

We leave for Rome as soon as I finish the short story I'm working on.

As Ever
Scott

I was interested that you've moved to New Canaan. It sounds wonderful. Sometimes I'm awfully anxious to be home.

---

[1] [Trimalchio was an ostentatious party giver in Petronius' *Satyricon*.—Ed.]

But I am confused at what you say about Gertrude Stien. I thought it was one purpose of critics + publishers to educate the public up to original work. The first people who risked Conrad certainly didn't do it as a commercial venture. Did the evolution of startling work into accepted work cease twenty years ago?

Do send me Boyds (Ernest's) book when it comes out. I think the Lardner ads are wonderful. Did the Dark Cloud flop?

Would you ask the people down stairs to keep sending me my monthly bill for the encyclopedia?

[c. December 1, 1924]
Hotel des Princes
Piazza di Spagna
Rome, Italy

Dear Max:

Your wire + your letters made me feel like a million dollars—I'm sorry I could make no better response than a telegram whining for money. But the long siege of the novel winded me a little + I've been slow on starting the stories on which I must live.

I think all your critisisms are true

(a) About the title. I'll try my best but I don't know what I can do. Maybe simply "Trimalchio" or "Gatsby." In the former case I don't see why the note shouldn't go on the back.

(b) Chapters VI + VII I know how to fix

(c) Gatsby's business affairs I can fix. I get your point about them.

(d) His vagueness I can repair by <u>making more pointed</u>—this doesn't sound good but wait and see. It'll make him clear

(e) But his long narrative in Chap VIII will be difficult to split up. Zelda also thought I was a little out of key but it is good writing and I don't think I could bear to sacrifice any of it

(f) I have 1000 minor corrections which I will make on the proof + several more large ones which you didn't mention.

Your critisisms were excellent + most helpful + you picked out all my favorite spots in the book to praise as high spots. Except you didn't mention my favorite of all—the chapter where Gatsby + Daisy meet.

Two more things. Zelda's been reading me the cowboy book aloud to spare my mind + I love it—tho I think he learned the American language from Ring rather than from his own ear.

Another point—in Chap. II of my book when Tom + Myrte go into the bedroom while Carraway reads Simon called Peter[2]—is that raw? Let me know. I think its pretty nessessary.

I made the royalty smaller because I wanted to make up for all the money you've advanced these two years by letting it pay a sort of interest on it. But I see by calculating I made it too small—a difference of 2000 dollars. Let us call it 15% up to 40,000 and 20% after that. That's a good fair contract all around.

By now you have heard from a smart young french woman who wants to translate the book. She's equeal to it intellectually + linguisticly I think—had read all my others—If you'll tell her how to go about it as to royalty demands ect.

Anyhow thanks + thanks + thanks for your letters. I'd rather have you + Bunny like it than anyone I know. And I'd rather have you like it than Bunny. If its as good as you say, when I finish with the proof it'll be perfect.

Remember, by the way, to put by some cloth for the cover uniform with my other books.

As soon as I can think about the title I'll write or wire a decision. Thank Louise for me, for liking it. Best Regards to Mr. Scribner. Tell him Galsworthy is here in Rome.

As Ever,

Scott

[c. December 20, 1924]
Hotel des Princes, Piazza de Spagna, Rome.

Dear Max:

I'm a bit (not very—not dangerously) stewed tonight + I'll probably write you a long letter. We're living in a small, unfashionable but most comfortable hotel at $525.00 a month including tips, meals ect. Rome does not particularly interest me but its a big year here, and early in the spring we're going to Paris. There's no use telling you my plans because they're usually just about as unsuccessful as to work as a religious prognosticaters are as to the End of the World. I've got a new novel to write—title and all, that'll take about a year. Meanwhile, I don't want to start it until this is out + meanwhile I'll do short stories for money (I now get

---

[2] [Fitzgerald regarded this popular 1921 novel by Robert Keable as immoral; the protagonist is an army chaplain who becomes involved in passionate episodes.—Ed.]

$2000.00 a story but I hate worse than hell to do them) and there's the never dying lure of another play.

Now! Thanks enormously for making up the $5000.00. I know I don't technically deserve it considering I've had $3000.00 or $4000.00 for as long as I can remember. But since you force it on me (inexecrable [or is it execrable] joke) I will accept it. I hope to Christ you get 10 times it back on Gatsby——and I think perhaps you will.

For:

I can now make it perfect but the proof (I will soon get the immemorial letter with the statement "We now have the book in hand and will soon begin to send you proof" [what is 'in hand'—I have a vague picture of everyone in the office holding the book in the right and and reading it]) will be one of the most expensive affairs since Madame Bovary. Please charge it to my account. If its possible to send a second proof over here I'd love to have it. Count on 12 days each way—four days here on first proof + two on the second. I hope there are other good books in the spring because I think now the public interest in books per se rises when there seems to be a group of them as in 1920 (spring + fall), 1921 (fall), 1922 (spring). Ring's + Tom's (first) books, Willa Cathers Lost Lady + in an inferior, cheap way Edna Ferber's are the only American fiction in over two years that had a really excellent press (say, since Babbit).

With the aid you've given me I can make "Gatsby" perfect. The chapter VII (the hotel scene) will never quite be up to mark—I've worried about it too long + I can't quite place Daisy's reaction. But I can improve it a lot. It isn't imaginative energy thats lacking—its because I'm automaticly prevented from thinking it out over again because I must get all those characters to New York in order to have the catastrophe on the road going back + I must have it pretty much that way. So there's no chance of bringing the freshness to it that a new free conception sometimes gives.

The rest is easy and I see my way so clear that I even see the mental quirks that queered it before. Strange to say my notion of Gatsby's vagueness was O.K. What you and Louise + Mr. Charles Scribner found wanting was that:

I myself didn't know what Gatsby looked like or was engaged in + you felt it. If I'd known + kept it from you you'd have been too impressed with my knowledge to protest. This is a complicated idea but I'm sure you'll understand. But I know now—and as a penalty for not having known first, in other words to make sure I'm going to tell more.

It seems of almost mystical significance to me that you thot he was older—the man I had in mind, half unconsciously, <u>was</u> older (a specific individual) and evidently, without so much as a definate word, I conveyed the fact.—or rather, I must qualify this Shaw-Desmond-trash by saying, that I conveyed it without a word that I can at present and for the life of me, trace. (I think Shaw Desmond was one of your bad bets—I was the other)

Anyhow after careful searching of the files (of a man's mind here) for the Fuller Magee case[3] + after having had Zelda draw pictures until her fingers ache I know Gatsby better than I know my own child. My first instinct after your letter was to let him go + have Tom Buchanan dominate the book (I suppose he's the best character I've ever done—I think he and the brother in "Salt" + Hurstwood in "Sister Carrie" are the three best characters in American fiction in the last twenty years, perhaps and perhaps not) but Gatsby sticks in my heart. I had him for awhile then lost him + now I know I have him again. I'm sorry Myrtle is better than Daisy. Jordan of course was a great idea (perhaps you know its Edith Cummings) but she fades out. Its Chap VII thats the trouble with Daisy + it may hurt the book's popularity that its <u>a man's book</u>.

Anyhow I think (for the first time since The Vegetable failed) that I'm a wonderful writer + its your always wonderful letters that help me to go on believing in myself.

Now some practical, very important questions. Please answer every one.

① Montenegro has an order called <u>The Order of Danilo</u>. Is there any possible way you could find out for me there what it would look like—whether a courtesy decoration given to an American would bear an English inscription—or anything to give versimilitude to the medal which sounds horribly amateurish.

② Please have <u>no blurbs of any kind on the jacket</u>!!! No Mencken or Lewis or Sid Howard or anything. I don't believe in them <u>one bit</u> any more.

③ Don't forget to change name of book in list of works

④ Please shift exclamation point from end of 3d line to end of 4th line in title page. <u>Please!</u> Important!

⑤ I thought that the whole episode (2 paragraphs) about their playing the Jazz History of the world at Gatsby's first party was rotten. Did you? Tell me frank reaction—<u>personal</u>. Don't <u>think</u>! We can all think! [. . .]

Always yours

Scott Fitz——

---

[3] [Edward M. Fuller and William F. McGee, partners in a stock brokerage firm, were convicted of embezzlement; Arnold Rothstein—the model for Meyer Wolfshiem in *The Great Gatsby*—was allegedly involved in their peculations.—Ed.]

Hotel des Princes
Rome, Italy
January 24.-1925
(But address the American Express
Co. because its damn cold here
and we may leave any day.

Dear Max:

This is a most important letter so I'm having it typed. Guard it as your life.
1) Under a separate cover I'm sending the first part of the proof. While I agreed with the general suggestions in your first letters I differ with you in others. I want Myrtle Wilson's breast ripped off—its exactly the thing, I think, and I don't want to chop up the good scenes by too much tinkering. When Wolfshiem says "sid" for "said", it's deliberate. "Orgastic" is the adjective from "orgasm" and it expresses exactly the intended ecstasy. It's not a bit dirty. I'm much more worried about the disappearance of Tom and Myrtle on galley 9—I think it's all right but I'm not sure. If it isn't please wire and I'll send correction.
2) Now about the page proof—under certain conditions never mind sending them (unless, of course, there's loads of time, which I suppose there isn't. I'm keen for late March or early April publication)
The conditions are two.
a) That someone reads it very carefully twice to see that every one of my inserts are put in correctly. There are so many of them that I'm in terror of a mistake.
b) That no changes whatsoever are made in it except in the case of a misprint so glaring as to be certain, and that only by you.

If there's some time left but not enough for the double mail send them to me and I'll simply wire O.K. which will save two weeks. However don't postpone for that. In any case send me the page proof as usual just to see.
3) Now, many thanks for the deposit. Two days after wiring you I had a cable from Reynolds that he'd sold two stories of mine for a total of $3,750. but before that I was in debt to him and after turning down the ten thousand dollars from College Humor[4] I was afraid to borrow more from him until he'd made a sale. I won't ask for any more from you until the book has earned it. My guess is that it will sell about 80,000 copies but I may be wrong. Please thank Mr. Charles Scribner for me. I bet he thinks he's caught another John Fox now for sure. Thank God for John Fox. It would have been awful to have had no predecessor.

---

[4] [For serialization of *The Great Gatsby*.—Ed.]

4) This is very important. Be sure not to give away <u>any</u> of my plot in the blurb. Don't give away that Gatsby <u>dies</u> or is a <u>parvenu</u> or <u>crook</u> or anything. It's a part of the suspense of the book that all these things are in doubt until the end. You'll watch this won't you? And remember about having no quotations from critics on the jacket—<u>not even about my other books</u>!

5) This is just a list of small things.

    a) What's Ring's title for his spring book?

    b) Did O'Brien star my story <u>Absolution</u> or any of my others on his trash-album?

    c) I wish your bookkeeping department would send me an account on Feb. 1st. Not that it gives me pleasure to see how much in debt I am but that I like to keep a yearly record of the sales of all my books.

Do answer every question and keep this letter until the proof comes. Let me know how you like the changes. I miss seeing you, Max, more than I can say.

As ever,

Scott

P.S. I'm returning the proof of the title page ect. It's O.K. but my heart tells me I should have named it <u>Trimalchio</u>. However against all the advice I suppose it would have been stupid and stubborn of me. <u>Trimalchio in West Egg</u> was only a compromise. <u>Gatsby</u> is too much like Babbit and <u>The Great Gatsby</u> is weak because there's no emphasis even ironically on his greatness or lack of it. However let it pass.

[c. February 18, 1925]

New Address { Hotel Tiberio
Capri

Dear Max:

After six weeks of uninterrupted work the proof is finished and the last of it goes to you this afternoon. On the whole its been very successful labor

    (1.) I've brought Gatsby to life

    (2.) I've accounted for his money

    (3.) I've fixed up the two weak chapers (VI and VII)

    (4.) I've improved his first party

    (5.) I've broken up his long narrative in Chap. VIII

This morning I wired you to <u>hold up the galley of Chap 40</u>. The correction—and God! its important because in my other revision I made Gatsby look too mean—is enclosed herewith. Also some corrections for the page proof.

We're moving to Capri. We hate Rome, I'm behind financially and have to write three short stories. Then I try another play, and by June, I hope, begin my new novel.

Had long interesting letters from Ring and John Bishop. Do tell me if all corrections have been recieved. I'm worried

Scott

I hope you're setting publication date at first possible moment.

[1925]
April 10th

Dear Max:

The book comes out today and I am overcome with fears and forebodings. Supposing women didn't like the book because it has no important woman in it, and critics didn't like it because it dealt with the rich and contained no peasants borrowed out of <u>Tess</u> in it and set to work in Idaho? Suppose it didn't even wipe out my debt to you—why it will have to sell 20,000 copies even to do that! In fact all my confidence is gone—I wouldn't tell you this except for the fact that by the this reaches you the worst will be known. I'm sick of the book myself—I wrote it over at least five times and I still feel that what should be the strong scene (in the Hotel) is hurried and ineffective. Also the last chapter, the burial, Gatsby's father ect is faulty. Its too bad because the first five chapters and parts of the 7th and 8th are the best things I've ever done.

"The best since Paradise". God! If you you knew how discouraging that was. That was what Ring said in his letter together with some very complementary remarks. In strictest confidence I'll admit that I was disappointed in <u>Haircut</u>—in fact I thought it was pretty lousy stuff—the crazy boy as the instrument of providence is many hundreds of years old. However please don't tell him I didn't like it.

Now as to the changes I don't think I'll make any more for the present. Ring suggested the correction of certain errata—if you made the changes all right—if not let them go. Except on Page 209 old dim La Salle Street Station should be <u>Union</u> old dim Union Station and should be changed in the second edition. Transit will do fine though of course I really meant compass. The page proofs arrived and seemed to be O.K. though I don't know how the printer found his way through those 70,000 corrections. The cover (jacket) came too and is a delight. Zelda is mad about it (incidently she is quite well again.

When you get this letter address me % Guaranty Trust Co. 1 Rue Des Italennes, Paris.

Another thing—I'm convinced that Myers is all right but have him be sure and keep all such trite phrases as "Surely the book of the Spring!" out of the advertiseing. That one is my pet abomination. Also to use no quotations <u>except those of unqualified and exceptionally entheusiastic praise from emminent individuals. Such phrases as</u>

"Should be on everyone's summer list"

Boston Transcript

"Not a dull moment . . . a thoroughly sound solid piece of work"

havn't sold a copy of any book in three years. I thought your advertising for Ring was great. I'm sorry you didn't get Wescotts new book. Several people have written me that <u>The Apple of the Eye</u> is the best novel of the year.

Life in New Cannan sounds more interesting than life in Plainfield. I'm sure anyhow that at least two critics Benet + Mary Column will have heard about the book. I'd like her to like it—Benet's opinion is of no value whatsoever.

And thanks mightily for the $750.00 which swells my debt to over $6000.00.

When should my book of short stories be in?

Scott

P. S.

I had, or rather saw, a letter from my uncle who had seen a preliminary announcement of the book. He said:

"it sounded as if it were very much like his others."

This is only a vague impression, of course, but I wondered if we could think of some way to advertise it so that people who are perhaps weary of assertive jazz and society novels might not dismiss it as "just another book like his others". I confess that today the problem baffles me—all I can think of is to say in general to avoid such phrases as "a picture of New York life" or "modern society"—though as that is exactly what the book is its hard to avoid them. The trouble is so much superficial trash has sailed under those banners. Let me know what you think

Scott

[c. April 24, 1925]
Marseille, en route to Paris

Dear Max:

Your telegram[5] depressed me—I hope I'll find better news in Paris and am wiring you from Lyons. There's nothing to say until I hear more. If the book fails commercially it will be from one of two reasons or both

1st The title is only fair, rather bad than good.

2nd <u>And most important</u>—the book contains no important woman character and women controll the fiction market at present. I don't think the unhappy end matters particularly.

It will have to sell 20,000 copies to wipe out my debt to you. I think it will do that all right—but my hope was it would do 75,000. This week will tell.

Zelda is well, or almost but the expense of her illness and of bringing this wretched little car of ours back to France which has to be done, by law, has wiped out what small progress I'd made in getting straight financially.

In all events I have a book of good stories for the fall. Now I shall write some cheap ones until I've accumulated enough for my my next novel. When that is finished and published I'll wait and see. If it will support me with no more intervals of trash I'll go on as a novelist. If not I'm going to quit, come home, go to Hollywood and learn the movie business. I can't reduce our scale of living and I can't stand this financial insecurity. Anyhow there's no point in trying to be an artist if you can't do your best. I had my chance back in 1920 to start my life on a sensible scale and I lost it and so I'll have to pay the penalty. Then perhaps at 40 I can start writing again without this constant worry and interruption

<u>Yours in great depression</u>
Scott

P.S. Let me know about Ring's Book. Did I tell you that I thought <u>Haircut</u> was mediochre?

P.S. (2) Please refer any movie offers to Reynolds.

---

[5] [Perkins cabled Fitzgerald on April 20: "Sales situation doubtful. Excellent reviews."—Ed.]

Glossary of Literary Terms

allegory A device in which characters and events stand for abstract ideas, principles, or forces, so that the literal situation suggests a deeper symbolic meaning.

alliteration The repetition of identical or nearly identical sounds at the beginning of consecutive or nearby words.

allusion A reference to a person, place, thing, or event, historical or fictional, that suggests a wider frame of reference or greater depth of meaning.

apostrophe A direct address to an inanimate object or an absent or deceased person.

climax The point of greatest intensity or complication in a narrative; the turning point in a plot or dramatic action.

connotation The ideas and feelings commonly associated with or suggested by a word.

elegy A formal and sustained lament on the death of a particular person (adj., elegiac).

epiphany A moment of sudden insight or enlightenment that provides a character with new understanding about himself or herself or about a situation.

foreshadowing An indirect suggestion or clues that predict events yet to unfold in a story.

hyperbole A figure of speech that uses exaggeration for emphasis or effect and can also reveal aspects of a character or situation that are not directly stated.

imagery The sensory details in a written work, both literal and figurative, that create vivid impressions and emotional suggestions.

irony The contrast between what is directly relayed (through speech or description) and what is actually meant, or a state of affairs that is the opposite of what is expected.

metaphor A figure of speech that involves an implied or direct comparison between two relatively unlike things.

motivation The reasoning or emotion that drives a character's actions.

objective correlative A term coined by T. S. Eliot to describe a set of objects, a chain of events, or a situation that evokes a particular emotion.

paradox An apparent contradiction that is often true under examination.

personification A figure of speech in which human characteristics are assigned to nonhuman things.

point of view The perspective from which a story is told, such as first person, third-person limited, and third-person omniscient.

protagonist The central character around which the story revolves.

rhetoric The art of persuasion; the use of specific devices to achieve the intellectual and emotional effects that will persuade an audience.

setting The environment in which a story takes place, which involves the entire landscape of geography, season, atmosphere, and mood.

simile A comparison between two unlike things using the word *like* or *as*.

symbol Something that is itself and also stands for something else.

synesthesia The description of one sense impression using vocabulary usually associated with another sense, as when sound is attributed to color.

syntax The combination of words into phrases, clauses, and sentences.

theme A central idea in a literary work.

tone The attitude or feeling that pervades a given work, as determined by word choice, style, imagery, connotation, sound, and rhythm.

understatement A figure of speech that uses restraint or indifference to achieve irony or rhetorical effect.

Selected Bibliography

Allen, Frederick Lewis. *Only Yesterday: An Informal History of the 1920s.* New York: Harper & Row, 1931.

Behr, Edward. *Prohibition: Thirteen Years That Changed America.* New York: Arcade Publishing, 1996.

Berman, Ronald. The Great Gatsby *and Modern Times.* Urbana, Ill.: University of Illinois Press, 1994.

Bruccoli, Matthew J. *Some Sort of Epic Grandeur: The Life of F. Scott Fitzgerald.* Revised edition. New York: Carroll & Graf, 1992.

Burns, Ric. *New York: A Documentary Film.* Episodes 5 and 6. New York: PBS Home Video, 1999.

Cowley, Malcolm. *A Second Flowering: Works and Days of the Lost Generation.* New York: Viking Press, 1973.

Douglas, Ann. *Terrible Honesty: Mongrel Manhattan in the 1920s.* New York: Farrar, Straus & Giroux, 1995.

Fitzgerald, F. Scott. *The Crack-Up.* Edited by Edmund Wilson. New York: New Directions, 1993.

———. *A Life in Letters: F. Scott Fitzgerald.* Edited by Matthew J. Bruccoli. New York: Simon & Schuster, Touchstone, 1995.

———. *The Letters of F. Scott Fitzgerald.* Edited by Andrew Turnbull. New York: Dell, 1963.

Hasse, John Edward, ed. *Jazz: The First Century.* New York: William Morrow, 2000.

The Marx-Engels Reader. 2d ed. Edited by Robert C. Tucker. New York: W. W. Norton, 1978.

Mizener, Arthur. *The Far Side of Paradise: A Biography of F. Scott Fitzgerald.* Boston: Houghton Mifflin, 1965.

Mowry, George E., ed. *The Twenties: Fords, Flappers, and Fanatics.* Englewood Cliffs, N.J.: Prentice-Hall, 1963.

Piper, Henry Dan. *Fitzgerald's* The Great Gatsby: *The Novel, the Critics, the Background.* New York: Charles Scribner's Sons, 1970.

Stevenson, Elizabeth. *Babbitts and Bohemians: The American 1920s.* New York: Macmillan, 1967.

Tate, Mary Jo. *F. Scott Fitzgerald A to Z: The Essential Reference to His Life and Work.* New York: Facts on File, 1998.

Acknowledgments

All possible care has been taken to trace ownership and secure permission for each selection in this book. The Great Books Foundation wishes to thank the following authors, publishers, and representatives for permission to reprint copyrighted material:

Winter Dreams, from BABYLON REVISITED AND OTHER STORIES, by F. Scott Fitzgerald. Copyright 1960 by Charles Scribner's Sons.

Passages from THE GREAT GATSBY, by F. Scott Fitzgerald. Copyright 1925 by Charles Scribner's Sons. Copyright renewed 1953 by Frances Scott Fitzgerald Lanahan. Editorial material copyright 1991, 1992 by Eleanor Lanahan, Matthew J. Bruccoli, and Samuel J. Lanahan as Trustees Under Agreement Dated July 3, 1975, Created by Frances Scott Fitzgerald Smith.

Coolidge Prosperity and *The Ballyhoo Years,* from ONLY YESTERDAY: AN INFORMAL HISTORY OF THE NINETEEN-TWENTIES, by Frederick L. Allen. Copyright 1931 by Frederick Lewis Allen. Copyright renewed 1959 by Agnes Rogers Allen. Reprinted by permission of HarperCollins Publishers, Inc.

The Flourishing of Jazz, from JAZZ: THE FIRST CENTURY, by John Edward Hasse, text only, pp. 26–27. Copyright 2000 by John Edward Hasse and Ted Lathrop. Reprinted by permission of HarperCollins Publishers, Inc.

The Evolution of the Flapper, from BABBITTS AND BOHEMIANS: THE AMERICAN 1920S, by Elizabeth Stevenson. Copyright 1967 by Elizabeth Stevenson. Reprinted with the permission of Scribner, a division of Simon & Schuster, Inc.

Playing Along the Danger Line: Women in the 1920s, from CENTURY OF WOMEN, by Sheila Rowbotham. Copyright 1997 by Sheila Rowbotham. Used by permission of Viking Penguin, a division of Penguin Putnam, Inc.

The Bootlegger, from THE TWENTIES: FORDS, FLAPPERS, AND FANATICS, edited by George Mowry. Copyright 1963 by Prentice-Hall, Inc.

Profile of a Bootlegger, from PROHIBITION: THIRTEEN YEARS THAT CHANGED AMERICA, by Edward Behr, published by Arcade Publishing. Copyright 1996 by Edward Behr.

Conspicuous Consumption, from THE THEORY OF THE LEISURE CLASS, by Thorstein Veblen, introduction by C. Wright Mills, pp. 68–101. Copyright 1953, renewed by New American Library. Used by permission of Dutton Signet, a division of Penguin Putnam, Inc.

Alienation and Social Classes, from "The Holy Family," by Karl Marx, translated by R. C. Tucker, from THE MARX-ENGELS READER, SECOND EDITION, by Robert C. Tucker. Copyright 1978, 1972 by W. W. Norton & Company, Inc. Used by permission of W. W. Norton & Company, Inc.

The Horatio Alger Myth, from SILAS SNOBDEN'S OFFICE BOY, by Horatio Alger. Copyright 1973 by Doubleday and Company. Used by permission of Doubleday, a division of Random House, Inc.

Selected Letters, from A LIFE IN LETTERS: F. SCOTT FITZGERALD, edited and annotated by Matthew J. Bruccoli. Copyright 1994 by the Trustees Under Agreement Dated July 3, 1975, Created by Frances Scott Fitzgerald Smith.

Photo and Art Credits